MW01592367

Instant Pot Whole 30 Cookbook

2018 Whole 30 Instant Pot Cookbook - with Healthy & Delicious Instant Pot Cooker Recipes

Dave Luckly

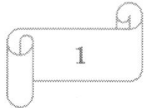

© Copyright 2017 –Dave - All Rights Reserved.

In no way is it legal to reproduce, duplicate, or transmit any part of this document by either electronic means or in printed format. Recording of this publication is strictly prohibited, and any storage of this material is not allowed unless with written permission from the publisher. All rights reserved.

The information provided herein is stated to be truthful and consistent, in that any liability, regarding inattention or otherwise, by any usage or abuse of any policies, processes, or directions contained within is the solitary and complete responsibility of the recipient reader. Under no circumstances will any legal liability or blame be held against the publisher for any reparation, damages, or monetary loss due to the information herein, either directly or indirectly. Respective authors own all copyrights not held by the publisher.

Legal Notice:
This book is copyright protected. This is only for personal use. You cannot amend, distribute, sell, use, quote or paraphrase any part or the content within this book without the consent of the author or copyright owner. Legal action will be pursued if this is breached.

Disclaimer Notice:

Please note the information contained within this document is for educational and entertainment purposes only. Every attempt has been made to provide accurate, up-to-date and reliable, complete information. No warranties of any kind are expressed or implied. Readers acknowledge that the author is not engaging in the rendering of legal, financial, medical or professional advice.

By reading this document, the reader agrees that under no circumstances are we responsible for any losses, direct or indirect, which are incurred as a result of the use of information contained within this document, including, but not limited to, errors, omissions, or inaccuracies.

Contents

Introduction

I would like to start off by expressing my utmost gratitude and appreciation to you and your kind gesture for purchasing and downloading my book.

I have tried my very best to make sure that this book is as much accessible and valuable to Whole30 readers as possible.

As such, the book has been carefully divided into multiple parts for you to easily digest and understand.

Since everything is in bite sized portions, you will be able to absorb the information easily and leisurely.

Throughout the book I will be discussing the core concepts of the Whole30 diet and teach you how to follow the diet from scratch. So, if you are an absolutely beginner, you will still be able to jump into the bang wagon!

And don't worry, I haven't forgotten about the Instant Pot part of the book! There is a brief chapter completely dedicated towards Instant Pot as well that gives you that teaches you the basics of the Pot itself.

I welcome you to your harmonious Whole30 Journey with your new and shiny Instant Pot!

Chapter 1: Understanding the Concept of Whole30

If you think about it, then the underlying principle of the Whole30 diet actually dates back to 2009 when it was first conceived by now, world famous medical practitioners Melissa and Dallas Hartwig.

Generally speaking, the core object of the Whole30 diet is to completely reset the internal metabolic system of the human body by restricting it from eating certain harmful food groups over a course of 30 days.

This meticulously planned out system allows the body to completely re-invigorate itself and improve the condition of your metabolic, digestive and also defensive mechanism of the body.

Even if it sounds difficult at first, trust me as your body will drastically improve in the long run.

What is Whole30 and The Whole30 Challenge?

If you are curious about the working procedure though, there is no secret formula behind the success of the diet!

By eliminating the certain food groups such as junk foods, dairy products, sugary products from your diet you are

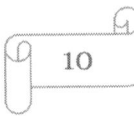

essentially relieving it from consuming harmful and unhealthy products.

This process of elimination allows your body to reassesses the internal mechanism of the body, which leads to a healthier body.

Due to this process, the Whole30 diet is also sometimes known as an "Elimination Diet"

To quote the founders and designers of the Whole30 program, "By eliminating all of the inflammatory, psychology unhealthy, gut-disrupting and hormone unbalancing foods groups for 30 days, the Whole30 diet will literally 'Change Your Life' forever!"

The Whole30 challenge is simply that! All you have to do is follow the strict diet of clean food for a period of 30 days.

But before you jump into your amazing Instant Pot Whole30 recipes, I would encourage you to walk through the introductory chapters before to get a good understanding of the concept as a whole.

Let starts with the basics first.

The Advantages of the Whole30

If you are new to the field of Whole30 then you are bound to be curious to know the various advantages and disadvantages of the diet right?

To summarize,

- If sugar is eliminated from your system, you will be able to get more sound and relaxing sleep.
- You'll be able to get a boost of consistent energy all throughout the day.
- You won't be facing any digestive problems such as stomach bloating, farts or tummy rumblings.
- You will be at peace and your anxiety levels will significantly lower down.
- The condition of your skin will vastly improve since you are going for more vegetables and protein while eliminating sugar altogether.
- Your hair will be healthier and shinier.
- Workout sessions will be more effective.
- Not to mention, aside from making you healthy! The Whole30 diet will actually help you to trim down those pesky body fats and give you a fine body image and attractive physique.

And believe me when I tell you that these are just the tip of the Ice Berg! Meaning, there's a whole lot of advantages down the road of the 30 days.

Allowed Whole30 Foods

The following are some of the food that you are allowed to eat while on a Whole30 diet.

- Almond flour
- Almond milk
- Arrowroot Powder
- Bacon
- Bean Sprouts
- Cacao
- Canola Oil
- Olive Oil
- Carob
- Chia
- Citric Acid
- Coconut Flour
- Coconut Water
- Coffee
- Dates
- Flax Seed
- Fruit Juice
- Guar Gum
- Green Beans
- Hemp Seeds
- Larabars
- Mayonnaise (Homemade)
- Mustard
- Nutritional Yeast
- Potatoes (Added in August 2014)
- Salt

- Sunflower Oil
- Snow Peas
- Tahini
- Water Kefir
- Egg

To elaborate, the following food groups are completely allowed:

- Vegetables
- Fruits
- Unprocessed Meat
- Seafood
- Nuts and Seeds
- Oils and Ghee

Restricted Food

Alternatively, these are the ones that you should steer clear from during the 30 days.

- Amino Acids
- Buckwheat
- Carob
- Deep Fried Chips
- Dark Chocolate
- Chewing Gum
- Hummus
- Paleo Bread
- Paleo Ice Cream
- Pancakes
- Any kind of Protein Shakes

- Quinoa
- Stevia Leaf
- Vanilla Extract

To elaborate, the food groups to avoid are:

- Dairy products such as cow milk, cream, yogurt, kefir, butter etc. (only clarified butter/ghee is allowed)
- Any kind of grains such as corn, wheat, quinoa, millet etc.
- Alcoholic Beverages
- Legumes such as peas, lentils, peanuts or even soy such as tofu, miso or Edamame

Some Minute Side Effects To Know About

In the long run, there are actually no side effects for the Whole30 diet, however, since your body is going through a large change, some minor signs and symptoms are to be expected.

It should be noted though that these symptoms will eventually go away after the first 14 days of the diet.

- Minor headaches
- Feeling of lethargy
- Sleepiness
- General Crankiness
- Brain Fog
- Food Cravings
- Minor Breakouts

- Minor Bloating

Tips on Directions make Your journey successful

The following tips will help you to ensure that you are having a pleasant and smooth Whole30 journey throughout the 30 days!

- Make sure that you have fully set up your mind and have committed yourself to the journey
- Instead of planning for the 30 days, you should plan out the first 2 weeks first. Breaking down the whole journey will make it easier for you.
- Clear out the house off any foods that are non-Whole30 compliant
- Plan the meals before hand
- Mix and match the schedule to create your very own perfect plan! You can also take help from the meal plan provided in this book as well.
- Make sure to set one day aside to prepare your meals ahead of time.
- Try to keep food related socializing events at a minimum
- The Whole30 community is full of inspiration stories and figures. If you ever start feeling left out, just browse the web and you will get a plethora of support materials.
- Try to keep yourself distracted from food cravings.
- And most importantly, never give up

What Comes After The Whole30?

This is a part where most Whole30 followers tend to feel confused. What does one do once the 30 days has passed?

Well, there are actually 3 more steps that are needed to be followed.

I will go through each of the steps individually, starting with

Step 2: Reintroduction

The second step of the diet is known as the "Reintroduction" part and this is extremely crucial to the complete Whole30 journey.

So, once you are done with the first step of the diet, which is the "Whole30" challenge, you are now tasked to make a meal plan for the upcoming 10 days where you will re-introduce some of the food groups that you have been missing out.

Throughout this gradual introduction of the food produces, you will be able to assess how each food group affects your metabolic levels and evaluate, which foods are healthy and suitable for you in the long run.

The plan of re-introduction will usually require you to re-introduce 1 food group at a time, to ensure that you are still heavily relying on your Whole30 diet.

The re-introduction phase is often seen as being a scientific trial that helps you asses which food groups is better for your body and which are not.

You should keep in mind though that you are not to experiment with multiple food groups at once! So, you can only experiment either peanut butter or jam, not both!

During this phase, you are to pay very close attention as to how the body reacts to the food groups and react accordingly.

A sample meal plan might look the one below:

Day 1: You may start off by trying to re-introduced legumes and evaluate how they work.

Day 4: After a 3 days trial run, select the legumes that you want to keep and move on to re-introducing Non-Gluten grains such as corn tortilla chips or white rice.

Day 7: This should be followed by an evaluation of Dairy products. Some cheese or ice creams are to be considered during this phase.

Day 10: Finally, you should evaluate Gluten –Containing Grains to see how they react to your body.

You should keep in mind though that through the whole process, you asked to stick to your Whole30 diet while only allowed the food that you are experiment with.

Step 3: Share the Experience You Earned

Ever since the conception of your diet, the Whole30 has followed a very strong community of thousands of people all around the world, which is full of extremely helpful people.

So, once you are done with your Whole30 Challenge, simply go out into the wild and share your experience to the community and the people all around.

Believe me, you have no idea just how much of an impact your story might make on someone else's life.

If you are feeling confused though, here are some pointers that should help you to write your story:

- How you brought control over your food eating habits
- How Whole30 helped to eliminate various symptoms or conditions
- How the biomarkers such as triglycerides, blood pressure or blood sugar level improved
- How a Whole30 diet helped you to trim down your weight and gain back your confidence
- How it helped to become pregnant
- How Whole30 helped you to be at Peace with yourself
- How you were able to transfer the Whole30 habits to other aspects of your life and so on...

Step 4: The Upcoming Journey

You should keep in mind that the end of your 30 days is not to be considered as the end of your Whole30 journey! But rather, you should look at it as being the beginning to a healthier life.

While you won't be able to eradicate the damage that you may have done in the past, but you can most definitely make sure that your body stays healthy in the coming days.

That being said, the following strategies should help you to continue following your Whole30 journey well beyond the 30 days.

- Keep focusing on your Whole30 based meals everything single day as long as you can without breaks or any kind of "Cheat Day". Should the lust for sugar come creeping back to you, go for something very minute, just enough to control the temptation. But don't give into it!
- However, should you stumble upon something that is just too irresistible or perhaps something that is culturally or religiously important to you, make a small exception and assess if the food is actually worth it. If it helps, then you can follow the below given that will greatly help you assess the food and decide if eating it would be a good idea.

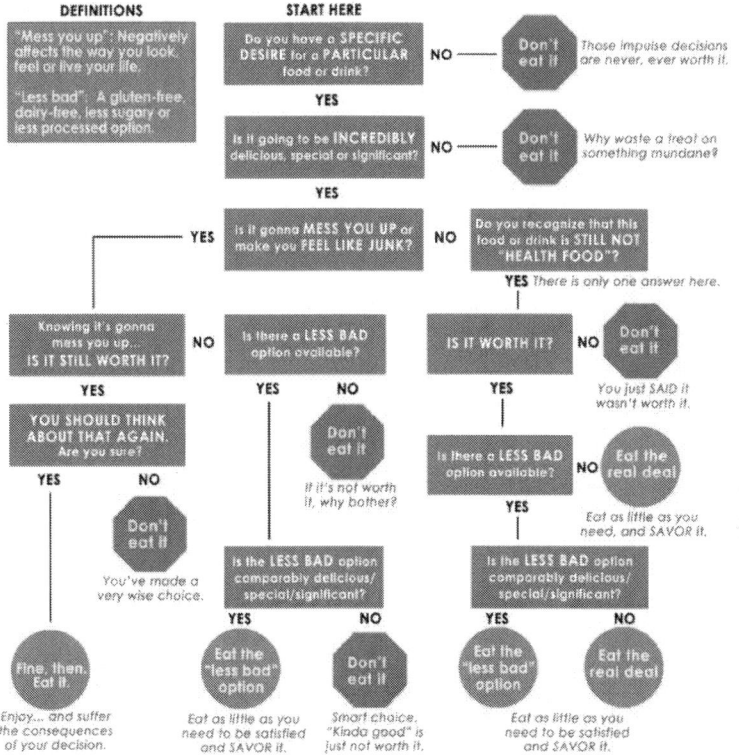

- Assuming that you have decided to let yourself go, make sure to take your time while eating the meal. Eat is consciously, trying to maintain your diet as much as you can. A good way to do this is to eat just as little as you need, until you are able to control your temptation. Once you are ready, keep the remaining for later use.

- Once you are done with your meal, make sure to not feel guilt or shame! What is done is done right? There's no turning back. So, it's better to just accept the fact that you have made a conscious decision and give yourself some slack. Try to keep yourself together and keep moving forward, trying to follow your Whole30 properly.

With that out of the way, since this book is focused on Whole30 recipes made Instant Pot, the second chapter of the book will focus a bit on explaining the basics of the Instant Pot device itself.

Chapter 2: Understanding the Fundamentals of the Instant Pot

I know that time is very important to you, and therefore without spending a lot of time on the intro, I am going to jump on the main point of the topic right away!

So, let's start with the most basic question now.

What is the Instant Pot?

Strictly speaking, the Instant Pot is a very versatile device that allows you to cook your meals utilizing the power of pressure cooking.

And on that topic, to get a better understanding of the mechanism behind Instant Pot, you should understand the meaning of "Pressure Cooking".

In the simplest terms, pressure cooking follows a very simple law of physics.

-   Boiling point of water increases as the pressure inside a sealed vessel increased

When it comes to an Instant Pot, as more and more steam is being generated inside, the pressure eventually increases. This leads to the water reaching very high temperatures

without actually boiling up or evaporating which helps the device to greatly minimize the time taken to prepare the meals.

Having a Look at the Anatomy of the Pot

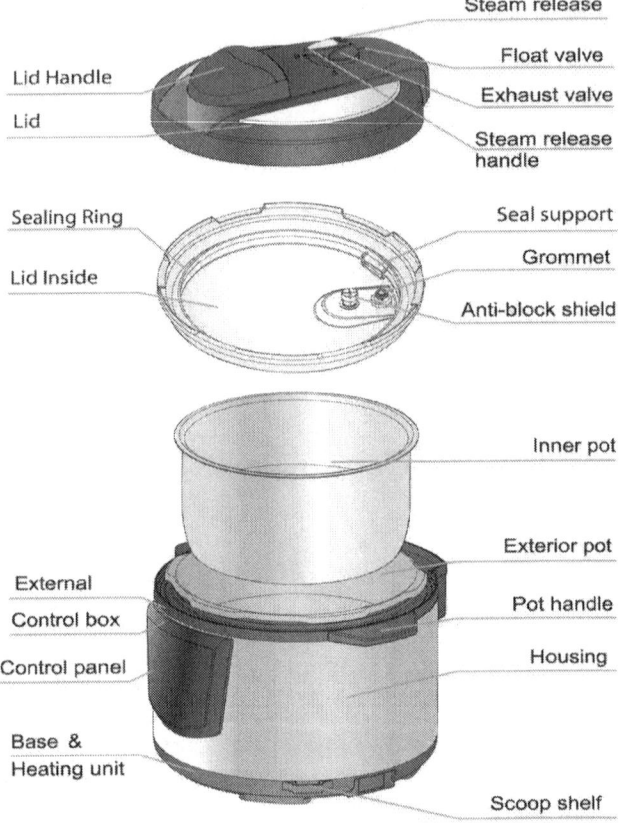

You should know that multiple electric pressure cooker manufacturing companies tend to apply something "unique" to make their pot more interesting, the following are the staple features of every pot.

- A cooker will have an inner pot which will also be known as a cooking pot
- There will be an electric heating element which acts as the heat source
- There will be sensors that will electronically control the pressure and temperature

The built in pressure and temperature sensors housed inside the device allows the pot to effortlessly monitor the internal environment and maintain optimal cooking conditions.

More advance Electric Pressure Cookers such as the Instant Pot even comes with pre-programmed settings which simply requires to user to select a setting based on what they are cooking, and the adjustments will be made automatically.

The accuracy of these various pre-programmed settings are very high as the settings were chosen after assimilating the data from a huge number of chefs all around the world.

Understanding the Different Buttons

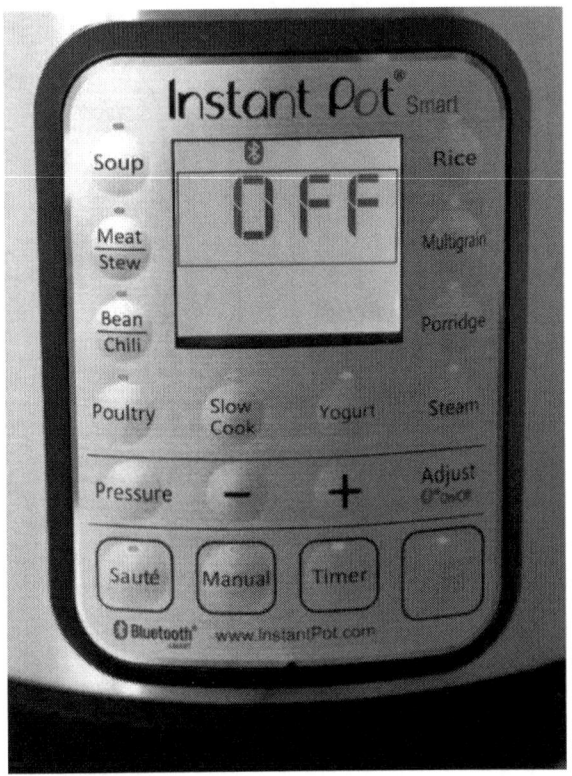

Due to the availability of a lot of buttons in the control panel, it is very common for individuals to feel confused or overwhelmed at times.

To ensure that the same thing does not happen to you, you just go through this section and it should make things a breeze for you.

- **Sauté:** You should go for this button if you want to simply sauté your vegetables or produces inside your inner pot while keeping the lid opened. It is possible to adjust the level of brownness you desire by pressing the adjust button as well. As a small tip here, you can very easily press the Sauté Button followed by the Adjust Button two times to simmer your food.

- **Keep Warm/Cancel:** Using this button, you will be able to turn your pressure cooker off. Alternatively, you can use the adjust button to keep maintaining a warm temperature ranging from 145 degree Celsius (at normal) to 167 (at more) degree Celsius depending on what you need.

- **Manual:** This is pretty much an all-rounder button which gives a greater level of flexibility to the user. Using this button followed by the + or - buttons, you will be able to set the exact duration of cooking time which you require.

- **Soup:** This mode will set the cooker to a high-pressure mode giving 30 minutes of cooking time (at normal); 40 minutes (at more); 20 minutes (at less)

- **Meat/Stew:** This mode will set the cooker to a high-pressure mode giving 35 minutes of cooking time (at normal); 45 minutes (at more); 20 minutes (at less)

- **Bean/Chili:** This mode will set the cooker to a high-pressure mode giving 30 minutes of cooking time (at normal); 40 minutes (at more); 25 minutes (at less)

- **Poultry:** This mode will set the cooker to a high-pressure mode giving 15 minutes of cooking time (at normal); 30 minutes (at more); 5 minutes (at less)

- **Rice:** This is a fully automated mode which cooks rice on low pressure. It will adjust the timer all by itself depending on the amount of water/rice present inside the inner cooking pot.

- **Multi-Grain:** This mode will set the cooker to a high-pressure mode giving 40 minutes of cooking time (at normal); 45 minutes (at more); 20 minutes (at less)

- **Porridge:** This mode will set the cooker to a high-pressure mode giving 20 minutes of cooking time (at normal); 30 minutes (at more); 15 minutes (at less)

- **Steam:** This will set your pressure cooker to high pressure with 10 minutes cooking time at normal. 15 minutes cook time at more and 3 minutes cook time at less. Keep in mind that it is advised to use this mode with a steamer basket or rack for best results.

- **Slow Cooker:** This button will normally set the cooker at 4-hour mode. However, you change the temperature by keeping it at 190-201 degree

Fahrenheit (at low); 194-205 degree Fahrenheit (at normal); 199-210 degree Fahrenheit (at high);

- **Pressure:** This button allows you to alter between high and low-pressure settings.

- **Yogurt:** This setting should be used when you are in the mood for making yogurt in individual pots or jars

- **Timer:** This button will allow you to either decrease or increase the time by using the timer button and pressing the + or – buttons.

The Different Parts of the Pot

The following are the different parts of the Instant Pot that you should know about.

The Cooking Pot

This is the internal part of the pot where the actual cooking takes place. In most cases the pot is usually carved out of Stainless Steel or Aluminum.

However, it is a good practice to look for cooking pots that are cladded with copper at the bottom. These allow the pot to evenly distribute the heat and cook more efficiently.

The Locking Mechanism

The Instant Pot has a Sealing Ring or "Gasket" that allows the pot to create a completely air tight chamber inside the vessel where the steam builds up and the cooking takes place.

Once the upper lid comes in contact with the inner pot, the vacuum layer is formed.

The Safety Mechanism of the pot

Since the Instant Pot deals with a lot of pressure, safety is always the first concert of the manufacturers.

The Instant Pot comes equipped with a very a unique mechanism known as the "Push Down Pressure Release" mechanism.

Push Down Pressure Release: The valves that are installed in the Instant Pot are designed with an innovative "Anti-Block Shield" that allows the valves to resist even the toughest and harshest conditions.

They are able to stay intact and locked up as long as the specified pressure has not been reached. However, once the pressure goes beyond the specified threshold, the seal position of the regulator valve pushes itself upward, which slowly release the pressure and returns it to acceptable levels.

The release valves are intelligently controlled with electronic sensors which determine the level and duration of the pressure build up, and alter the settings depending on the type of meal that you are cooking.

How the Optimal Conditions Are Maintained

As you may have already understood, the Instant Pot is a very versatile device and uses an intelligent software to control the various cooking parameters.

To break them down, these are:

- **The Heating Intensity:** The heating intensity of an instant pot is referring to the amount of heat created by the heating element at the bottom of the pot. The reason why the heating intensity is needed to be managed is because if the temperature goes out of control, then the food content at the bottom of the pot will start burning. When the pot is set in the soup mode, usually the intensity of the pot depends on the mode selected. For example, in the soup mode the heating is slow and gradual while it is pretty steep and fast in steam.
- **Temperature:** This is the temperature of the cooking pot in the pot throughout the whole process. Usually the maximum working temperature of the cooking pot falls in the region of 115 – 118 degree Celsius. The smart cooking program doesn't always hold the maximum temperature though, it intelligently alters temperature as required.
- **Pressure:** The pressure in an Instant Pot is the lifeblood of the cooking in this device. Whenever the liquid in this device reaches its boiling point, the pressure level rises as the steam becomes to generate which helps to rapidly cook the meal. The

thermodynamics of gas represents that the situation for such a product is ideal when the pressure and volume of the gas are directly proportion to the temperature produced. In this device, the volume remains constant so the pressure is ultimately what helping to further increase the temperature.

- **Duration of Cooking:** This is basically the period of time for which the food will be cooked. The duration of cooking usually is determined by the volume of food that are being cooked. For example, an approximation would that about 2 cups of rice takes almost 8 minutes of pressure time to cook. All of the pre-programmed timings are lab tested and perfectly work in almost all situations. It should be noted though that the instant pot has a nice feature called "Adjust" which allows you to manually adjust the duration

The Advantages of the Pot

Now that you are properly familiarized with the pot, it is time for you to understand the advantages of using the Pot! After all , you have to brag right?

- **Save both energy and time:** Since the pot is able to cook meals almost 70% faster when compared to other meals and cooking methods, this process greatly minimizes the time taken. Since the pot is insulated properly, it also helps to minimize energy loss and lower down energy consumption.

-

- **Preserve the nutrients of the food while keeping things tasty:** Unlike the other cooking methods out there, the Instant Pot just requires to have enough water to produce the steam required for the meal, instead of requiring the produces to be submerged completely. This helps to prevent the vitamins and all essential minerals from the vegetables and other produces to wash away.
- **Kills of harmful Micro-Organism:** Various raw produces are marred by different harmful microorganisms that might be harmful to the human body. In electric pressure cookers, the water level is heated to a high temperature where it reaches its boiling point. At this level, most if not all of the harmful micro-organisms are killed off. Wheat, rice, beans and corns carry fungal poisons such as Aflatoxins which might even lead to live cancer. Recent Korean studies have concluded that cooking food under pressure was successfully able to bring down the levels of Aflatoxins to a very satisfactory level.

The Basics of Using the Pot

While some people still think that using the Instant Pot is really tough, the truth is actually the complete opposite!

Even if you arc an absolute beginner, you will be able to master the device in no time!

But first, the two things that you should know about are :

"How the meals are cooked" and "How the pressure is released"

Now one thing you should keep in mind is that the processes that are used in this book are known as "Water Test"

- Open up the lid of your Instant Pot
- Add a 1 or 2 cups of water into the inner pot of your Instant Pot
- Gently, move the valve to sealing position

- Select your pressure cooker timing, just use the manual button to set it to 5 minutes
- And that's it! Now all you have to do is just wait until the timer runs out! Within 5 minutes, the water should be heated up enough to have produced a good level of pressure

Next comes to the process of releasing the pressure.

There are actually two ways through which the pressure can be released.

- **Quick Release:** This method is suitable for ingredients such as vegetables.

- **Natural Release:** This method of releasing the pressure is best suited for ingredients such as meat.

Chapter 3: Chicken Recipes

Healthy Lettuce "Taco"

<u>Serves</u> 5

<u>Prep Time:</u> 5 minutes

<u>Cook Time:</u> 10 minutes

Ingredients

- 2 pound of boneless and skinless chicken breast
- 1 teaspoon of chili powder + ½ a teaspoon of kosher salt
- 1 cup of roasted tomato salsa
- Grain free tortillas/ lettuce wraps

Directions

1. *Carefully arrange the chicken in a single layer in your Instant Pot*
2. *Season them with salt (both sides)*
3. *Pour Salsa on top of the chicken pieces and lock up the lid*
4. *Cook on HIGH pressure for 7 minutes (for breast) or 10 minutes (for thigh) over high pressure*
5. *Release the pressure naturally once done*
6. *Remove the lid and transfer the chicken to a bowl*

7. *Shred them up and serve the chicken by assembling them on your lettuce wraps*

8. *Enjoy!*

Nutrition Values (Per Serving)

- Calories: 407
- Fat: 32g
- Carbohydrates: 13g
- Protein: 20g

Freshly Prepped Pinna Colada Chicken

Serves 4

Serves 4

Prep Time: 15 minutes

Cook Time: 15 minutes

Ingredients

- 2 pound of organic chicken thigh
- 1 cup of fresh pineapple chunks
- ½ a cup of coconut cream
- 1 teaspoon of cinnamon
- 1/8 teaspoon of salt
- 2 tablespoon of coconut aminos
- ½ a cup of chopped up green onion

Directions

1. Add all of the listed ingredients to your pot with the exception of the green onion
2. Lock up the lid and cook on HIGH pressure for 15 minutes
3. Once done, release the pressure naturally
4. Take a bowl and mix arrowroot flour and a tablespoon of water to a make slurry
5. Stir this slurry into your pot and make a thick mixture
6. Set your pot to Saute and keep cooking until you have a thick mixture
7. Garnish with some green onion and serve!

Nutrition Values (Per Serving)

- Calories: 358
- Fats: 12g
- Carbs:20g
- Fiber: 3g

The Whole30 Compliant Authentic Shredded Chicken

<u>Serves</u> 6

<u>Prep Time:</u> 4 minutes

<u>Cook Time:</u> 20 minutes

Ingredients

- 4 pounds of chicken breast
- ½ a cup of chicken broth
- 1 teaspoon of salt
- ½ a teaspoon of black pepper

Directions

1. Add all of the listed ingredients to your pot and give it a nice stir
2. Lock up the lid and cook on HIGH pressure for 20 minutes
3. Release the pressure naturally
4. Take the chicken out and transfer it to a cutting board
5. Shred it using fork
6. Serve immediately and enjoy!

Nutrition Values (Per Serving)

- Calories: 395
- Fat: 14g
- Carbohydrates: 40g
- Protein: 28g

A Perfect Chicken Marsala

<u>Serves</u> 5

<u>Prep Time:</u> 10 minutes

<u>Cook Time:</u> 20 minutes

Ingredients

- 2 pound of boneless chicken breast
- 1 teaspoon of coconut oil
- 2 cloves of minced garlic
- 1 cup of sliced shitake mushrooms
- 1 cup of Marsala cooking wine
- ½ a cup of organic chicken broth
- 3 tablespoon of unflavored gelatin
- Large spaghetti squash
- Salt as needed
- Pepper as needed
- Fresh basil

Directions

1. Place the steamer rack on top of your pot

2. Add 1 cup of water and add the spaghetti squash to the rack

3. Seal up the lid and allow it to cook on high pressure for 20 minutes

4. Allow it to release the pressure naturally

5. Discard the water and allow the pot to dry

6. Set the pot to Saute mode and add coconut oil

7. Add salt, chicken and pepper

8. Sear until browed

9. Top with garlic, Marsala and mushrooms

10. Lock up the lid and cook for about 7-8 minutes on high pressure

11. Release the pressure naturally

12. Stir the chicken broth into the pot and allow it to warm

13. Remove ¼ cup of the liquid

14. Add gelatin/cornstarch to the cup of liquid

15. Once dissolved, add the slurry back to the pot

16. Mix well

17. Cut up your squash in half and scoop out the seeds

18. Separate the squash from the rind

19. Arrange the noodles on your plate and top it up with chicken, Marsala sauce and mushrooms

20. Garnish with a bit of fresh basil

21. Enjoy!

Nutrition Values (Per Serving)

- Calories: 628
- Fat: 29g
- Carbohydrates: 16g
- Protein: 66g

Unique Liguria Chicken

Serves 4

Prep Time: 10 minutes

Cook Time: 15 minutes

Ingredients

- 2 chopped up garlic cloves
- 3 sprigs of fresh rosemary
- 2 sprigs of fresh sage
- ½ a bunch of parsley
- 3 pieces of lemon completely juiced
- 4 tablespoon of extra virgin olive oil
- 1 teaspoon of sea salt
- ¼ a teaspoon of pepper
- 1 and ½ cup of water
- 1 whole piece of chicken, preferably cut into parts
- 3.5ounce of black gourmet salt-cured olives
- 1 fresh lemon

Directions

1. Take a bowl and add chopped up garlic, rosemary, sage and parsley
2. Take a bowl and add olive oil, lemon juice and mix well
3. Season it with pepper and salt

4. Remove the chicken skin from the chicken pieces and transfer them to a separate dish

5. Pour the marinade on top of the chicken pieces and allow it to chill for 2-4 hours

6. Set your pot to Saute mode and add olive oil, allow the oil to heat up

7. Add the chicken and brown them

8. Measure out marinade and add to the pot, making sure to cover the chicken pieces. If needed, you may add a bit of water as well

9. Lock up the lid and cook on HIGH pressure for 10 minutes

10. Release the pressure naturally over 10 minutes

11. Cover with a foil and allow them to cool

12. Set your pot in Saute mode and reduce the liquid to ¼

13. Add the chicken pieces again to the pot and allow them to warm

14. Sprinkle a bit of olives, lemon slices and rosemary

15. Enjoy!

Nutrition Values (Per Serving)

- Calories: 994
- Fats: 86g
- Carbs:15g
- Fiber:2g

Mind-Bobbling Mexican Chicken Cacciatore

<u>Serves</u> 4

<u>Prep Time:</u> 5 minutes

<u>Cook Time:</u> 10 minutes

Ingredients

- Extra virgin olive oil
- 3 chopped up shallots
- 4 crushed garlic cloves
- 1 seeded and sliced green bell pepper
- ½ a cup of organic chicken broth
- 10 ounce of sliced mushroom
- 5-6 pieces of skinless chicken breast
- 2 cans of organic crushed tomatoes
- 2 tablespoon of Organic Tomato Paste
- 1 can of pitted black olive
- Some fresh parsley
- Red pepper as required
- Salt as required
- Black pepper as required

Directions

1. *Set your pot to Saute mode and add oil, allow the oil to heat up*
2. *Add shallots, bell pepper and cook for 2 minutes*

3. *Add broth and allow it to reach boil, keep cooking for 2-3 minutes more*
4. *Add garlic, mushroom and the chicken*
5. *Cover with crushed tomatoes and the tomato paste*
6. *Lock up the lid and cook for 8 minutes over HIGH pressure*
7. *Release the pressure naturally and stir in parsley, pepper flakes, pepper and serve hot!*

Nutrition Values (Per Serving)

- Calories: 518
- Fat: 37g
- Carbohydrates: 10g
- Protein: 32g

Healthy Whole30 Chicken Yum Yum

<u>Serves</u> 6

<u>Prep Time:</u> 5 minutes

<u>Cook Time:</u> 18-40 minutes

Ingredients

- 2 pound of fresh boneless chicken thigh
- 3 tablespoon of homemade ketchup
- 1 and a ½ teaspoon of salt
- 2 teaspoon of garlic powder
- ¼ cup of ghee
- ½ teaspoon of finely ground black pepper
- 3 tablespoon of gluten free organic tamari
- ¼ cup of date paste

Directions

1. *Add the listed ingredients to your pot and stir well to make sure that the chicken is coated evenly*
2. *Lock up the lid and cook on HIGH pressure for 18 minutes*
3. *Once cooked, do a quick release*
4. *Transfer the chicken to your cutting board and shred it up*
5. *Set your pot to Saute mode and cook for 5 minutes until the juice has been reduced*
6. *Pour the sauce over the chicken and serve!*

Nutrition Values (Per Serving)

- Calories: 165
- Fat: 11.1g
- Carbohydrates: 5.1g
- Protein: 13g

Vegetable Chicken Breast Pieces

Serves: 4

Prep Time: 10 minutes

Cook Time: 40 minutes

Ingredients

- ½ of a Chicken breast
- 2 cups of carrots
- 8 medium sized new potatoes
- 1 cup of pearl onion
- ½ a cup of chicken broth
- 1 spring rosemary
- 1 pieces of spring thyme
- 2 pieces of minced cloves of garlic
- 1 teaspoon of salt
- 1 teaspoon of black pepper

Directions

1. Season the chicken breast with salt and pepper
2. Grease the Instant Pot with olive oil
3. Pour broth
4. Stir well and add the chicken breast
5. Add layers on garlic ,onion, thyme rosemary and top them up
with potatoes and carrots
6. Season well

7. Lock up the lid and cook on MEAT mode for 40 minutes

8. Allow the pressure to release naturally

9. Broil the chicken for 5 minutes if you prefer a crispier chicken

10. Enjoy!

Nutritional Values (Per Serving)

- Calories : 232
- Fat : 17g
- Carbohydrates : 0g
- Protein : 18

Refreshing Mango Chicken

6

Prep Time: 5 minutes

Cook Time: 15 minutes

Ingredients

- 4 pieces of chicken breast
- 14 ounce of mango chunky salsa
- 1 piece of fresh mango
- Jamaican hot sauce
- Salt as needed

Directions

1. *Add a cup of water to the pot*
2. *Season the chicken breast with salt*
3. *Place a steamer rack on top of your pot and add the chicken breast*
4. *Top the chicken breast with half of the Salsa*
5. *Lock up the lid and cook on HIGH pressure for 15 minutes*
6. *Release the pressure naturally and remove the chicken*
7. *Drain the liquid from the pot and transfer the chicken back to your pot (with no steamer this time)*
8. *Add hot sauce and shred the chicken*
9. *Dice the mango and add it to the pot*
10. *Serve and enjoy!*

Nutritional Values (Per Serving)

- Calories : 720
- Fat : 42g
- Carbohydrates : 16g
- Protein : 66g

Snacking Garlic and Chicken Bites

<u>Serves</u> 4

<u>Prep Time:</u> 10 minutes

<u>Cook Time:</u> 10 minutes

Ingredients

- 1 pound of ground chicken meat
- 1 cup of almond flour
- 3 pieces of beaten egg
- 2 tablespoon of garlic powder
- 1 tablespoon of black pepper

Directions

1. *Take a bowl and add the listed ingredients to the bowl*
2. *Mix them well*
3. *Add a cup of water to your pot*
4. *Take an oven safe dish and line it up with parchment paper*
5. *Place the mix in the dish*
6. *Take an aluminum foil and cover it up*
7. *Transfer it to your pot and lock up the lid*
8. *Cook for about 10 minutes at HIGH pressure*
9. *Release the pressure naturally, take the meat out and form patties. Enjoy!*

Nutritional Values (Per Serving)

- Calories: 240

- Fat: 15g
- Carbohydrates: 12g
- Protein: 14g

Generic Curried Chicken Potato Meal

<u>Serves</u> 4

<u>Prep Time:</u> 10 minutes

<u>Cook Time:</u> 25 minutes

Ingredients

For Marinade

- 4 pound of chicken legs
- 1 teaspoon of garlic powder
- 1 teaspoon of onion powder
- 1 tablespoon of spicy yellow curry powder
- 2 tablespoon of olive oil
- 1 teaspoon of kosher salt

For Curry

- 2 cups of coconut milk
- 1 tablespoon of spicy yellow curry powder
- 1 cup of water
- 4 cups of peeled potatoes cut up into 1.5 inch chunks
- ¼ cups of chopped dates
- ¼ cup of chopped cilantro
- ¼ cup of sliced fresh jalapenos

Directions

1. Take a large sized bowl and add the ingredients listed under Marinade
2. Mix well
3. Add the chicken and toss it well
4. Allow it to sit overnight
5. Set your pot to Saute mode and add chicken and brown it
6. Add 2 cups of coconut milk, 1 tablespoon of yellow curry powder, ¼ cup of dates , 4 cups of potato to the pot
7. Lock up the lid and cook on HIGH pressure for 25 minutes
8. Release the pressure naturally once done,
9. Transfer the chicken to a serving plate (with potatoes) and simmer the liquid over Saute mode to thicken it
10. Pour the sauce over the chicken and garnish with a bit of cilantro
11. Enjoy!

Nutrition Values (Per Serving)

- Calories: 501
- Fat: 29g
- Carbohydrates: 24g
- Protein: 31g

Tantalizing Turkey Dish

<u>Serves</u> 6

<u>Prep Time:</u> 15 minutes

<u>Cook Time:</u> 60 minutes

Ingredients

- 1 piece of 4-5 pound bone-in skin on turkey breast
- Salt as needed
- Black pepper as needed
- 2 tablespoon of ghee
- 1 medium sized onion cut up into medium dice
- 1 large sized carrot cut up into medium dice
- 1 celery rib cut up into medium dice
- 1 garlic clove peeled and smashed
- 2 teaspoon of dried sage
- 1 and a ½ cup of bone broth
- 1 bay leaf
- 1 tablespoon of tapioca starch

Directions

1. Pat your breast dry carefully and season it with pepper and salt
2. Melt your butter in the instant pot over Saute mode
3. Add the turkey breast and allow it to brown for about 5 minutes, remove the breast to a plate

4. Add onion, celery, carrot to the pot and Saute them for about 5 minutes

5. Stir in sage and garlic and Saute them for 30 seconds

6. Pour wind and cook for about 3 minutes until slightly reduced

7. Stir in bay leaf, broth and scrape out the brown bits using a wooden spoon

8. Add the turkey with the skin side facing up

9. Lock up the lid and let it cook for 35 minutes at high pressure

10. Quick release the pressure once done

11. Transfer the breast to a carving plate and tent it with a foil

12. Let it rest for a while

13. Take an immersion blender and transfer the cooking liquid (from pot) alongside the vegetables and to a bowl and puree them until smooth

14. Return the mixture to the pot and allow it to cook until it has thickened

15. Once done, slice up the turkey and serve it with the gravy

Nutrition Values (Per Serving)

- Calories: 325
- Fat: 13g
- Carbohydrates: 0g
- Protein: 49g

Very Cool Rotisserie Chicken

<u>Serves</u> 6

<u>Prep Time:</u> 5 minutes

<u>Cook Time:</u> 25 minutes

Ingredients

- 1 whole chicken
- 1 and a ½ teaspoon of salt
- 1 teaspoon of granulated garlic
- ½ a teaspoon of pepper
- 1 and ¾ tablespoon of avocado oil
- 1 yellow quartered onion
- 1 halved lemon
- 1 cup of chicken broth

Directions

1. Remove the chicken cavity parts and rinse them well

2. Pat your chicken dry with a paper towel

3. Take a small ramekin dish and add spices, pepper and salt

4. Give it a nice stir and add oil and stir well

5. Set your pot to Saute mode

6. Rub the breast with oil and the spice mix

7. Transfer the chicken breast to your pot and brown it for 3-4 minutes until fully crisp

8. Flip the breast and cook for 1 minute more

9. Add chicken stock and lock up the lid

10. Cook on HIGH pressure for *25* minutes and allow the pressure to release naturally

11. Remove the lid and transfer the chicken to your serving plate

12. Allow it to rest for about *5* minutes and serve by pouring a bit of the cooking liquid

Nutrition Values (Per Serving)

- Calories: 649
- Fat: 48g
- Carbohydrates: 24g
- Protein: 35

Cranberry and Balsamic Chicken Delight

Serves: 4

Prep Time: 5 minutes

Cook Time: 35 minutes

Ingredients

- 2 pounds of chicken thigh skinless and boneless
- Salt as needed
- Pepper as needed
- 1 piece of copped up red onion
- ¼ cup of water
- 1 cup of cranberry sauce
- 3 tablespoon of balsamic vinegar
- 1 tablespoon of Worcestershire sauce
- 1 tablespoon of coconut aminos
- ½ a tablespoon of garlic powder
- ½ a tablespoon of rosemary
- 1 tablespoon of cornstarch

Directions

1. Spray the Instant Pot with Whole30 compliant cooking spray or oil

2. Set the pot to Saute mode and allow the oil to heat up

3. Season the thigh with pepper and salt and transfer to the pot

4. Brown them well for about 4-5 minutes, cook in batches if needed

5. Add chopped up onion to the pot and Saute until caramelized

6. Add ¼ cup of water and work around using a spatula to scrape off drippings

7. Take a small sized mixing bowl and add cranberry sauce, balsamic vinegar, aminos, rosemary, Worcestershire sauce, garlic powder and give it a nice mix

8. Lock up the lid and cook on HIGH pressure for 15 minutes

9. Quick release the pressure

10. Remove the chicken and transfer it to a platter

11. Add a mixture of 1 tablespoon of water and 1 tablespoon of cornstarch to the sauce for a thicker mixture

12. Saute for 2-3 minutes if adding the mixture and pour the gravy over the thigh

13. Enjoy!

Nutritional Values (Per Serving)

- Calories : 421
- Fat : 7g
- Carbohydrates : 60g
- Protein : 30g

Ghee Dredged Chicken Meal

<u>Serves</u> 4

<u>Prep Time:</u> 15 minutes

<u>Cook Time:</u> 17 minutes

Ingredients

- 2-3 pound of boneless chicken thigh
- 1 tablespoon of ghee
- 1 and ½ large onion completely chopped
- 3 and a ½ teaspoon of salt
- 2 teaspoon of garlic powder
- 2 teaspoon of ginger powder
- 2 heaping teaspoon of turmeric
- 1 and a ½ teaspoon of cayenne powder
- 1 and a ½ cup of stewed tomatoes
- 370 ml of tomato paste
- 2 cans of coconut milk
- 2 heaping teaspoon of Garam masala
- ½ a cup of slice almond
- ½ a cup of cilantro

Directions

1. Set your pot to Saute mode and add ghee, allow the ghee to heat up
2. Add 2 teaspoon of salt alongside onion and cook it

3. Add garlic, ginger, turmeric, paprika, cayenne pepper and mix well

4. Add the canned tomatoes, coconut milk and mix well

5. Add chicken and give it a nice stir

6. Lock up the lid and cook on HIGH pressure for 8 minutes

7. Release the pressure naturally

8. Pour coconut cream, Garam Masala and tomato paste

9. Garnish with a bit of cilantro and sliced up almonds

10. Enjoy!

Nutrition Values (Per Serving)

- Calories: 384
- Fats: 2g
- Carbs:8g
- Fiber:2g

Chapter 4: Seafood Recipes

The Mediterranean "Tuna" Zoodles

<u>Serves:</u> 8

<u>Prep Time:</u> 5 minutes

<u>Cook Time:</u> 10 minutes

Ingredients

- 1 tablespoon of oil
- ½ a cup of chopped up red onion
- 8 ounce of zucchini zoodles
- 1 can of diced tomatoes, basil, garlic , oregano
- 1 and a ¼ cup of water
- ¼ teaspoon of salt
- 1/8 teaspoon of pepper
- 1 can of tuna fish
- 1 jar of marinated artichoke hearts
- Freshly chopped up parsley

Direction

1. *Set the pot to Saute mode and add red onions*
2. *Cook them for 2 minutes*
3. *Add Zoodles, salt, tomatoes and pour the water*
4. *Lock up the lid and cook on HIGH pressure for 10 minutes*
5. *Release the pressure naturally over 10 minutes*

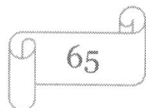

6. Open up the lid and add artichokes, tuna *with liquid) and set your pot to Saute mode
7. Keep stirring for 5 minutes
8. Serve and enjoy!

Nutritional Values (Per Serving)

- Calories: 125
- Fat: 8g
- Carbohydrates: 15g
- Protein: 6g

Priceless Salmon with Vegetables

<u>Serves</u> 4

<u>Prep Time:</u> 5 minutes

<u>Cook Time:</u> 10 minutes

Ingredients:

For Fish

- 2 medium sized salmon fillets
- 1 clove of finely diced garlic
- ¼ long red chili finely diced
- Sea salt as needed
- Pepper as needed
- 1 teaspoon of date paste
- 2 tablespoon of coconut aminos

For Veggies

- 7 ounce of mixed green vegetables
- 1 large sized sliced carrot
- 1 diced clove of garlic
- Juice of ½ a lime
- 1 tablespoon of tamari sauce
- 1 tablespoon of olive oil
- ½ a teaspoon of sesame oil

Direction

1. Add 1 cup of water to your pot and place a steamer rack on top
2. Add fillets to a heat proof bowl and sprinkle diced garlic, garlic and chili on top
3. Season with some salt and pepper
4. Take a small sized bowl and add date paste, tamari sauce and pour the mixture over the fillets
5. Take a small bowl and add date paste, tamari sauce and pour mixture over your fillets
6. Set the salmon bowl in the steamer rack and lock up the lid
7. Cut the vegetables accordingly and place them in a steam basket, season with some salt
8. Once the timer runs out, release the pressure quickly
9. Transfer the steam basket with the veggies on top of your salmon bowl
10. Drizzle the veggies with lime juice, olive oil, tamari sauce, sesame oil and season with a bit of salt and pepper
11. Lock up the lid and set timer to 0 and high pressure, wait for a minute and quick release the pressure
12. Remove the steamer basket with veggies and keep it on the side
13. Remove the bowl the salmon and transfer it to your plate
14. Pour any leftover juice on top and serve with the veggies

Nutrition Values (Per Serving)

- Calories: 236
- Fat: 15g
- Carbohydrates: 0g

- Protein: 023g

Salmon and Orange Medley

<u>Serves</u> 4

<u>Prep Time:</u> 10 minutes

<u>Cook Time:</u> 15 minutes

Ingredients

- 4 pieces of salmon fillets
- 1 cup of orange juice
- 2 tablespoon of cornstarch juice
- 1 teaspoon of grated orange peel
- 1 teaspoon of black pepper

Directions

1. *Add all of the listed ingredients to your pot*
2. *Lock up the lid and cook on HIGH pressure for 12 minutes*
3. *Release the pressure naturally*
4. *Open and serve!*

Nutrition Values (Per Serving)

- Calories:583
- Fat: 20g
- Carbohydrates: 71g
- Protein: 33g

Cute Swordy Fish Of Garlic

<u>Serves</u> 6

<u>Prep Time:</u> 10 minutes

<u>Cook Time:</u> 180 minutes

Ingredients

- 5 sword fish fillets
- ½ a cup of melted clarified butter
- 6 chopped up garlic cloves
- 1 tablespoon of black pepper

Directions

1. *Take a mixing bowl and add garlic, black pepper and clarified butter*
2. *Take a parchment paper and add your cod fillet*
3. *Cover with the mixture and wrap up the fish*
4. *Keep repeating until all the fish have been wrapped up*
5. *Allow them to cook for 2 and a ½ hour at high pressure*
6. *Release the pressure naturally*
7. *Serve and enjoy!*

Nutrition Values (Per Serving)

- Calories: 379
- Fat: 26g
- Carbohydrates: 1g
- Protein: 34g

Gently Steamed Salmon Fillets

<u>Serves</u> 2

<u>Prep Time:</u> 10 minutes

<u>Cook Time:</u> 10 minutes

Ingredients

- 2 pieces of salmon fillets
- ¼ cup of chopped up onion
- 2 stalks of chopped up green onion stalk
- 1 egg
- Almond meal as needed
- Salt as needed
- Pepper as needed
- 2 tablespoon of olive oil

Directions

1. *Add a cup of water to your pot and place a steamer rack on top*
2. *Place the fish*
3. *Season the fish with salt and pepper and lock up the lid*
4. *Cook on HIGH pressure for 3 minutes*
5. *Once done, quick release the pressure*
6. *Remove the fish and allow it to cool*
7. *Break the fillets into a bowl and add egg, yellow and green onions*
8. *Add ½ a cup of almond meal and mix with your hand*
9. *Divide the mixture into patties*
10. *Take a large skillet and place it over medium heat*

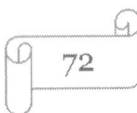

11. Add oil and cook the patties

12. Enjoy!

Nutrition Values (Per Serving)

- Calories: 238
- Fat: 15g
- Carbohydrates: 1g
- Protein: 23g

Fascinating Tilapia Curry

Serves 4

Prep Time: 10 minutes

Cook Time: 8 minutes

Ingredients

- 1 pound of tilapia fillets cut up in 2 inch pieces
- 1 tablespoon of olive oil
- ½ a teaspoon of mustard seed
- 1 can of coconut milk
- 1 tablespoon of ginger garlic paste
- 10-15 pieces of curry leaves
- ½ of a sliced medium onion
- ½ of a sliced green pepper
- ½ of a sliced yellow pepper
- 1 teaspoon of salt
- ½ a teaspoon of turmeric powder
- ½ a teaspoon of red chili powder
- 2 teaspoon of coriander powder
- 1 teaspoon of cumin powder
- ½ a teaspoon of Garam Masala
- 2-3 sprigs of cilantro
- 6-8 mint leaves
- ½ a teaspoon of lime juice

Directions

1. *Cut up the Tilapia into 2 inch pieces*

2. Slice up the onion and bell pepper and finely chop up the ginger-garlic and prepare the paste
3. Set your pot to Saute mode and add olive oil, allow the oil to heat up
4. Add mustard seeds and allow it to splutter, ad curry leaves, ginger garlic paste and Saute for about 30 seconds
5. Add sliced up onions, bell pepper and Saute for 30 seconds
6. Add spices and stir for 30 seconds more
7. Add coconut milk and bring it to a simmer, for 30 seconds
8. Add tilapia (cut up into 2 inch pieces) alongside a few cilantro sprigs and stir well to coat them up with the coconut milk
9. Add a few minute leaves on top
10. Lock up the lid and cook on HIGH pressure for 2-3 minutes
11. Do a quick release and serve!

Nutrition Values (Per Serving)

- Calories: 280
- Fat: 19g
- Carbohydrates: 4g
- Protein: 24g

Widely Renowned Coconut Fish Curry

Serves 4

Prep Time: 5 minutes

Cook Time: 5 minutes

Ingredients

- 1 can of coconut milk
- Juice of lime
- 1 tablespoon of red curry paste
- 1 teaspoon of fish sauce
- 1 teaspoon of coconut aminos
- 1 teaspoon of date paste
- 2 teaspoon of Sriracha
- 2 minced cloves of garlic
- 1 teaspoon of ground turmeric
- 1 teaspoon of ground ginger
- ½ a teaspoon of sea salt
- ½ a teaspoon of white pepper
- 1 pound of sea bass/cod cut up into 1 inch cubes
- ¼ cup of chopped fresh cilantro
- 3 pieces of lime wedges

Directions

1. Take a large sized bowl and add coconut milk, lime juice, red curry paste, fish sauce, date paste, coconut aminos, garlic sriracha, ginger, turmeric, white pepper, sea salt

2. Mix well
3. Place the sea bass/cod in the bottom of your Instant Pot
4. Pour coconut milk mix over the fish and lock up the lid
5. Cook for 3 minutes, do a quick release
6. Transfer the fish and broth into three individual bowls and garnish them with chopped up cilantro
7. Serve and enjoy!

Nutrition Values (Per Serving)

- Calories: 276
- Fat: 21g
- Carbohydrates: 4g
- Protein: 18g

Mediterranean –Styled Fancy Cod

<u>Serves</u> 4

<u>Prep Time:</u> 10 minutes

<u>Cook Time:</u> 6 minutes

Ingredients

- 6 pieces of fresh/frozen cod
- 3 tablespoon of clarified butter
- 1 juiced lemon
- 1 sliced up onion
- 1 teaspoon of salt
- ½ a teaspoon of black pepper
- 1 teaspoon of oregano
- 1 can of 28 ounce diced tomatoes

Directions

1. Set your pot to Saute mode and add the clarified butter
2. Once the butter is hot, add the remaining ingredients and give it a nice stir
3. Saute for 10 minutes
4. Arrange the fish portions in the sauce and use your spoon to cover the pieces with the sauce
5. Lock up the lid and cook on HIGH pressure for 5 minutes
6. Do a quick release and serve with the sauce
7. Enjoy!

Nutrition Values (Per Serving)

- Calories: 301
- Fat: 14g
- Carbohydrates: 14g
- Protein: 47g

Simple Sock Eye Salmon

<u>Serves</u> 4

<u>Prep Time:</u> 5 minutes

<u>Cook Time:</u> 5 minutes

Ingredients

- 3-4 ounce of Alaskan Sockeye Salmon Fillets
- 1 cup of water
- 2 cups of sliced lemons
- Salt as needed
- Pepper as needed

Directions

1. Add the steamer basket to your pot
2. Add 1 cup of water
3. Lay the fish on your steamer rack
4. Season with salt and pepper
5. Place lime slices on top
6. Lock up the lid and steam for 5 minutes
7. Quick release the pressure and serve over vegetables
8. Enjoy!

Nutrition Values (Per Serving)

- Calories: 487
- Fat: 20g
- Carbohydrates: 0g

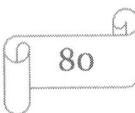

- Protein: 77g

An Instant Pot Instant Bowl of Shrimp

<u>Serves</u> 4

<u>Prep Time:</u> 5 minutes

<u>Cook Time:</u> 5 minutes

Ingredients

- 2 pound of shrimp
- 2 tablespoon of oil
- 2 tablespoon of clarified butter
- 1 tablespoon of minced garlic
- ½ a cup of white grape juice
- ½ a cup of chicken stock
- 1 tablespoon of lemon juice
- Parsley for garnish
- Salt as needed
- Pepper as needed

Directions

1. Add olive oil and clarified butter to your pot
2. Set the pot to Saute mode and add garlic, cook until a nice fragrance comes out
3. Add grape juice and chicken stock and deglaze the pot
4. Cancel the SAUTE mode and add shrimp
5. Lock up the lid and cook on MEAT/STEW more for 1 minute and naturally release the pressure
6. Open the lid and stir in lemon juice, pepper and salt

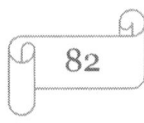

7. *Mix well and serve over some cauliflower rice if you prefer*
8. *Enjoy!*

Nutrition Values (Per Serving)

- Calories: 181
- Fat: 12g
- Carbohydrates: 2g
- Protein: 16g

Chapter 5: Pork Recipes

The Instant Pork Ragu

<u>Serves</u> 4

<u>Prep Time:</u> 5 minutes

<u>Cook Time:</u> 45 minutes

Ingredients

- 18 ounce of pork tenderloin
- 1 teaspoon of kosher salt
- Black pepper as needed
- 1 teaspoon of olive oil
- 5 cloves of garlic
- 1 can of 28 ounce crushed tomatoes
- 1 small sized jar of roasted red peppers
- 2 sprigs of thyme
- 2 pieces of bay leaves
- 1 tablespoon of chopped up fresh parsley divided

Directions

1. *Set your pot to Saute mode and season the pork with pepper and salt*
2. *Add oil to your pot and allow the oil to heat up*
3. *Add garlic and Saute for 1 and a ½ minute*

4. *Remove the garlic with a slotted spoon*
5. *Add pork to the pot and brown for 2 minutes on either sides*
6. *Add the remaining ingredients alongside garlic (make sure to reserve half of your kale for later use)*
7. *Lock up the lid and cook on HIGH pressure for 45 minutes*
8. *Once done, release the pressure naturally over 10 minutes and discard the bay leaves*
9. *Shred the pork using fork and garnish with parsley. Serve and enjoy!*

Nutrition Values (Per Serving)

- Calories: 93
- Fats: 1.5g
- Carbs:6g
- Fiber:1g

Pork Loin Chops with Pears

<u>Serves</u> 4

<u>Prep Time:</u> 5 minutes

<u>Cook Time:</u> 12 minutes

Ingredients

- 2 tablespoon of clarified butter
- 4 pieces of ½ inch t hick bone-in pork loin or rib chops
- ½ a teaspoon of salt
- ½ a teaspoon of ground black pepper
- 2 medium sized yellow onions peeled up and cut into 8 wedges
- 2 large Bosc pears, peeled up, cored and cut into 4 wedges
- ½ cup of unsweetened pear, cider
- ½ a teaspoon of ground allspice
- Several dashes of hot pepper

Directions

1. The first step here is to set your pot to sauté mode and melt in 1 tablespoon of butter
2. Toss your chops into your pot and cook for 4 minutes
3. Transfer the chops to a plate and repeat to cook and brown the rest

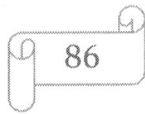

4. Toss in your onion and pears in your pot and let it cook for 3 minutes for until the pears are lightly browned

5. Pour in the cider the and stir the allspice, pepper sauce

6. Nestle the chops in your sauce

7. Lock up the lid and let it cook for about 10 minutes at high pressure

8. Quick release the pressure

9. Keep it there for 10 minutes to steam up your rice

10. Unlock and serve

Nutrition Values (Per Serving)

- Calories: 318
- Fat: 19g
- Carbohydrates: 4g
- Protein: 31g

Artichoke and Lemon "Thick" Pork Chops

<u>Serves</u> 4

<u>Prep Time:</u> 5 minutes

<u>Cook Time:</u> 24 minutes

Ingredients

- 2 tablespoon of clarified butter
- 2 pieces of 2 inch t hick bone-in pork loin or rib chops
- 3 ounce of pancetta diced of chunks
- 2 teaspoon of ground black pepper
- 1 medium sized minced up shallots
- 4 pieces of 2 inch lemon zest strips
- 1 teaspoon of dried rosemary
- 2 teaspoon of minced garlic
- 1 piece of 9 ounce box of frozen artichoke heart quarters
- ½ a cup of white grape juice
- ¼ cup of chicken broth

Directions

1. Set your pot to Saute mode and add the pancetta, cook for about 5 minutes
2. Transfer the browned up pancetta to a plate
3. Season the chops with pepper and transfer the chops to your pot

4. Cook until browned and remove the chops to a plate

5. Add shallots and cook for 1 minute

6. Add lemon zest, garlic, rosemary and stir until a nice aroma is released

7. Stir in broth and the artichokes and transfer back the pancetta as well

8. Transfer back the chops as well

9. Lock up the lid and let it cook for about 24 minutes at high pressure

10. Release pressure quickly

11. Unlock and transfer the chops to a carving board

12. Slice up the eye of your meat off the bone and slice the meat into strips

13. Divide in serving bowls and sauce ladled up

Nutrition Values (Per Serving)

- Calories: 245
- Fat: 45g
- Carbohydrates: 12g
- Protein: 48g

The Pork Meal Straight from Cuba

<u>Serves:</u> 10

<u>Prep Time:</u> 60 minutes

<u>Cook Time:</u> 80 minutes

Ingredients

- 3 pound of boneless pork shoulder blade roast, fat trimmed and removed
- 6 pieces of garlic cloves
- 2/3 cup of grapefruit juice
- ½ a tablespoon of fresh oregano
- ½ a tablespoon of cumin
- Juice of 1 lime
- 1 tablespoon of kosher salt
- 1 piece of bay leaf
- Lime wedges as needed
- Chopped up cilantro as needed
- Hot sauce as needed
- Salsa as needed

Directions

1. Cut up the pork into 4 pieces and transfer them to a bowl
2. Take a small sized blender and add garlic, oregano lime, grapefruit,, salt, cumin and blend the mixture well to form the marinade

3. Pour the marinade over your pork and allow it to rest for 60 minutes

4. Transfer the mix to the Instant Pot and add bay leaf

5. Lock up the lid and cook on HIGH pressure for 80 minutes

6. Release the pressure naturally

7. Remove the pork and shred it

8. Return the pork back to the pot

9. Add 1 cup of water and season with some liquid

10. Set it to Saute mode and cook for a few minutes

11. Enjoy once done!

Nutritional Values (Per Serving)

- Calories : 213
- Fat : 9g
- Carbohydrates : 2g
- Protein : 26g

A Ghee-Licious Pork Chop

<u>Serves</u> 4

<u>Prep Time:</u> 5 minutes

<u>Cook Time:</u> 15 minutes

Ingredients

- 2 tablespoon of clarified butter
- 4 pieces of ½ inch t hick bone-in pork loin or rib chops
- ½ a teaspoon of salt
- ½ teaspoon of ground black pepper
- 16 baby carrots
- 1 tablespoon of minced fresh dill fronds
- ½ a cup of white grape juice
- ½ a cup of chicken broth

Directions

1. Set your pot to Saute mode
2. Season the pork chop well with pepper and salt
3. Add the chop to your pot and cook for 4 minutes
4. Transfer the cooked chop to a plate (if needed, cook the chops in batches)
5. Pour 1 tablespoon of ghee to the pot alongside carrots, dill and cook for 1 minute
6. Add ½ a cup of grape juice and deglaze the pot
7. Stir in broth and add the chops

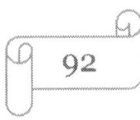

8. Lock up the lid and cook for 18 minutes over HIGH pressure

9. Naturally release the pressure

10. Serve by pouring the cooking sauce on top of the chops

Nutrition Values (Per Serving)

- Calories: 296
- Fat: 25g
- Carbohydrates: 0g
- Protein: 17g

Embedded Pork Shoulder Meal

<u>Serves</u> 6

<u>Prep Time:</u> 5 minutes

<u>Cook Time:</u> 60 minutes

Ingredients

- ¼ cup of orange juice
- ¼ cup of lime juice
- 5 minced garlic cloves
- 1 teaspoon of salt
- ½ a teaspoon of ground cumin
- 3 pound of boneless pork shoulder cut up into 2 inch cubes
- Chopped up fresh cilantro

Directions

1. Add orange juice, cumin, lime juice, garlic and salt to your pot
2. Add pork to the pot and toss well to cover it up
3. Lock up the lid and cook on HIGH pressure for 45 minutes
4. Allow the pressure to release naturally over 10 minutes
5. Pre-heat your broiler
6. Take the pork out using tong and place it on a baking sheet
7. Set the pot to Saute mode and allow the liquid to reduce for about 10-15 minutes

8. *Pour liquid into a heatproof dish*
9. *Broil your pork for about 3-5 minutes per side until crispy and serve the broiled pork with the sauce. Enjoy!*

Nutrition Values (Per Serving)

- Calories: 378
- Fat: 19g
- Carbohydrates: 0g
- Protein: 48g

Lovely Pulled Pork Meal

<u>Serves</u> 6

<u>Prep Time:</u> 7 minutes

<u>Cook Time:</u> 60 minutes

Ingredients

- 4 pound of pork roast
- 2 tablespoon of olive oil
- 1 head butter lettuce
- 2 grated carrot
- 2 wedge cut limes
- Water

For the spice mixture

- 1 tablespoon of cocoa powder
- 1 tablespoon of salt
- 1 tablespoon of red pepper flakes
- 2 teaspoon oregano
- 1 teaspoon of white pepper
- 1 teaspoon of garlic powder
- 1 teaspoon of cumin
- 1/8 teaspoon of coriander
- 1/8 teaspoon of cayenne pepper
- 1 large finely chopped up onion

Directions

1. *Take a bowl and add the ingredients listed under "Spice", mix them well*
2. *Season the roast with the prepared mixture and allow the seasoned roast to chill in your fridge overnight*
3. *Set your pot to Saute mode and add olive oil, allow the oil to heat up*
4. *Add meat and brown it well*
5. *Add water to submerge the meat*
6. *Lock up the lid and cook on HIGH pressure for 50-60 minutes*
7. *Release the pressure naturally*
8. *Take out the meat shred the flesh from the bones*
9. *Set your pot to Saute mode and reduce the liquid by simmering it*
10. *Add the shredded pork meat to a pan over medium heat and stir fry them until slightly brown*
11. *Add some olive oil and spices*
12. *Serve the fried pork pieces with the sauce*
13. *Enjoy!*

Nutrition Values (Per Serving)

- Calories: 176
- Fats: 7g
- Carbs:1.3g
- Fiber:5g

Interesting Kalua Pork

<u>Serves</u> 8

<u>Prep Time:</u> 5 minutes

<u>Cook Time:</u> 100 minutes

Ingredients

- 1 piece 4-5 pound of pork shoulder
- 1 tablespoon of bacon fat
- 1 teaspoon of salt
- ½ a cup of diced up pine apple
- 1 teaspoon of fish sauce
- 1 tablespoon of liquid smoke
- ½ a cup of water

Directions

1. Set your pot to Saute mode
2. Cut up the pork into two pieces and add bacon fat to the pot
3. Add shoulders and sear for about 2-3 minutes on each side to brown them
4. Sprinkle a bit of salt on top
5. Add fish sauce, pineapple, liquid smoke and water to the pot and stir
6. Lock up the lid and cook on HIGH pressure for 90 minutes
7. Release the pressure naturally

8. Remove the pork and to a platter and shred it using a fork
9. Pour the sauce over the pork and serve. Enjoy!

Nutrition Values (Per Serving)

- Calories: 357
- Fat: 28g
- Carbohydrates: 0g
- Protein: 25g

Very Juicy Apple Pork Tenderloins

<u>Serves</u> 4

<u>Prep Time:</u> 5 minutes

<u>Cook Time:</u> 30 minutes

Ingredients

- 2 tablespoon of clarified butter
- 3 pound of boneless pork loin roast
- 1 large red onion halved and thinly sliced
- 2 medium sized tart green apple
- 4 fresh thyme sprigs
- 2 bay leaves
  ¼ cup of chicken broth
- ½ teaspoon of salt
- ½ teaspoon of ground black pepper

Directions

1. Set your pot to Saute mode and add the butter

2. Allow the butter to heat up and add tenderloin pieces, cook for 8 minutes

3. Transfer the cooked loins to a serving platter

4. Add onions and Saute for 3 minutes

5. Stir in thyme, bay leaves and apple

6. Pour broth and stir in pepper and salt

7. Nestle the loin back in the pot and pour juice from the plate

8. Lock up the lid and cook on HIGH pressure for 30 minutes

9. Release the pressure naturally

10. Remove the lid and discard the bay leaf

11. Transfer the pork to a cutting board and allow it to sit for 5 minutes

12. Serve with the sauce in the pot

13. Enjoy!

Nutrition Values (Per Serving)

- Calories: 123
- Fat: 45g
- Carbohydrates: 43g
- Protein: 21g

Nice Pineapple Dredge Pork Chops

<u>Serves:</u> 4

<u>Prep Time:</u>10 minutes

<u>Cook Time:</u> 25 minutes

Ingredients

- 6 pieces of thin cut pork chops (bone-in)
- Balsamic glaze as needed
- Seasoning of your choice for the pork chops
- Olive oil as needed
- Cubed up pineapple

Directions

1. Season the chops well

2. Set the pot to Saute mode and add olive oil

3. Once the oil is hot, add the chops and Saute them

4. Remove the chops and layer them on a steamer rack (fir for the pot)

5. Glaze the upper part of the chop and add the pineapple chunks on top

6. Add a cup of water

7. Place the steamer rack on your pot

8. Lock up the lid and cook for 25 minutes under HIGH pressure

9. Release the pressure naturally and remove the chops

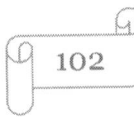

10. *Serve with a bit of pineapple glaze*

11. *Enjoy!*

Nutritional Values (Per Serving)

- Calories : 621
- Fat : 15g
- Carbohydrates : 101g
- Protein : 24g

Pulled Apart Pork Carnitas

<u>Serves</u>: 6

<u>Prep Time</u>: 7 minutes

<u>Cook Time</u>: 60 minutes

Ingredients

- 4 pound of pork roast
- 2 tablespoon of olive oil
- 1 head butter lettuce
- 2 grated carrot
- 2 wedge cut limes
- Water

For the spice mixture

- 1 tablespoon of cocoa powder
- 1 tablespoon of salt
- 1 tablespoon of red pepper flakes
- 2 teaspoon oregano
- 1 teaspoon of white pepper
- 1 teaspoon of garlic powder
- 1 teaspoon of cumin
- 1/8 teaspoon of coriander
- 1/8 teaspoon of cayenne pepper
- 1 large finely chopped up onion

Directions

1. Take a bowl and add the ingredients listed under "Spice", mix them well

2. Season the roast with the prepared mixture and allow the seasoned roast to chill in your fridge overnight

3. Set your pot to Saute mode and add olive oil, allow the oil to heat up

4. Add meat and brown it well

5. Add water to submerge the meat

6. Lock up the lid and cook on HIGH pressure for 50-60 minutes

7. Release the pressure naturally

8. Take out the meat shred the flesh from the bones

9. Set your pot to Saute mode and reduce the liquid by simmering it

10. Add the shredded pork meat to a pan over medium heat and stir fry them until slightly brown

11. Add some olive oil and spices

12. Serve the fried pork pieces with the sauce

13. Enjoy!

Nutrition Values (Per Serving)

- Calories: 176
- Fats: 7g
- Carbs:1.3g
- Fiber:5g

Chapter 6: Beef Recipes

Very Effective "Goulash"

<u>Serves</u> 6

<u>Prep Time:</u> 10 minutes

<u>Cook Time:</u> 15 minutes

Ingredients

- 1 -2 pound of extra lean ground beef
- 2 teaspoon of olive oil + additional 11 teaspoon
- 1 large sized red bell pepper, stemmed and seeded (cut up into short strips)
- 1 large sized onion cut up into short strips
- 1 tablespoon of minced garlic
- 2 tablespoon of sweet paprika
- ½ a teaspoon of hot paprika
- 4 cups of beef stock
- 2 cans of petite diced tomatoes

Directions

1. Set your pot to Saute mode and add 2 tablespoon of olive oil
2. Add ground beef to the pot and keep cooking and stirring until it breaks

3. Once the beef is browned up, transfer it to another bowl

4. Cut up the stem off the pepper and deseed them

5. Cut them up into strips

6. Cut the onions into short strips

7. Add teaspoon of olive oil to the pot and add onion and pepper

8. Add minced garlic, hot paprika, sweet paprika, and cook for 2-3 minutes

9. Add beef stock and tomatoes

10. Add ground beef and lock up the lid

11. Cook on LOW pressure for 15 minutes on SOUP mode

12. Quick release and enjoy!

Nutrition Values (Per Serving)

- Calories: 283
- Fat: 13g
- Carbohydrates: 13g
- Protein: 30g

Plain and Simple Beef Short Ribs

Prep Time: 10 minutes

Cook Time: 15 minutes

Ingredients

- 4 pound of beef short ribs
- Generous amount of Kosher Salt
- 1 tablespoon of beef fat
- 1 quartered onion with its skin on
- 3 cloves of garlic
- Water

Directions

1. Season the beef ribs well by rubbing salt all over
2. Take a skillet and place it over medium heat
3. Add oil and allow the oil to heat up
4. Add the ribs and brown them
5. Add garlic, onion and water (water level should be 2 inch below the top of the skillet rim)
6. Transfer the mixture to your Instant Pot
7. Give it a stir and lock up the lid
8. Cook on HIGH pressure for 35 minutes
9. Release the pressure naturally over 10 minutes
10. Enjoy!

Nutrition Values (Per Serving)

- Calories: 440
- Fats: 41g
- Carbs:10g
- Fiber:2g

Easy To Make Beef Stew

Serves 6

Prep Time: 10 minutes

Cook Time: 35 minutes

Ingredients

- 16 ounce of tenderloin cut
- 1 piece of chopped onion
- 1 chopped zucchini
- 3 Yukon gold potatoes chopped up
- 1 cup of chopped carrots
- 2 cups of beef broth
- 1-2 teaspoon of sea salt
- 1 piece of bay leaf
- 1 teaspoon of pepper
- 1 teaspoon of paprika
- 1 teaspoon of onion powder
- 1 tablespoon of tomato paste
- 2 tablespoon of arrowroot flour
- Worcestershire sauce

Directions

1. *Set your pot to Saute mode and add tenderloin alongside oil*
2. *Saute them until the meat is cooked well (no longer pink)*
3. *Add the vegetables and stir in broth alongside seasoning*

4. Lock up the lid and set your pot to "STEW/MEAT" mode
5. Cook for 35 minutes
6. Once done, release the pressure naturally and set your pot to WARM
7. Ladle ¼ of the liquid into a separate bowl and mix arrowroot flour
8. Stir in the slurry back the pot and stir to thicken the stew
9. Season with a bit of salt and enjoy!

Nutrition Values (Per Serving)

- Calories: 310
- Fat: 8g
- Carbohydrates: 18g
- Protein: 39g

Authentic Beef Bourguignon

<u>Serves</u> 4

<u>Prep Time:</u> 10 minutes

<u>Cook Time:</u> 30 minutes

Ingredients

- 1 pound of stewing steak
- ½ a pound of bacon
- 5 medium sized carrots
- 1 large peeled and sliced red onion
- 2 minced cloves of garlic
- 2 teaspoon of rock salt
- 2 tablespoon of fresh Thyme
- 2 tablespoon of fresh parsley
- 2 teaspoon of ground black pepper
- ½ a cup of beef broth
- 1 tablespoon of olive oil

Directions

1. *Set your pot to Saute mode and add 1 tablespoon of oil*
2. *Allow the oil to heat up and add beef (in batches) and brown them*
3. *Slice up the cooked bacon into strips and add the strips alongside onion to your pot*
4. *Add the rest of the ingredients and give it a nice stir*
5. *Lock up the lid and cook on HIGH pressure for 30 minutes*

6. Release the pressure naturally and enjoy!

Nutrition Values (Per Serving)

- Calories: 416
- Fats: 18g
- Carbs: 12g
- Fiber: 3g

Vietnamese Bo Kho

Serves 4

Prep Time: 10 minutes

Cook Time: 50 minutes

Ingredients

- ½ a teaspoon of ghee
- 2 and a half pound of grass fed beef brisket
- 1 yellow onion all peeled up and diced
- 1 and a ½ teaspoon of curry powder
- 2 and a ½ tablespoon of peeled up fresh ginger
- 2 cups of drained and crushed, diced up tomatoes
- 3 tablespoon of red boat fish sauce
- 2 tablespoon of applesauce
- 1 large stalk of lemongrass with the loose leaves trimmed off and cut into 3 inch pieces while being bruised with a meat pounder
- 2 whole sized star anise
- 1 piece of bay leaf
- 1 cup of bone broth

Directions

1. Set your pot to Saute mode and add ghee, allow the ghee to heat up
2. Add briskets and fry until they have a nice brown texture
3. Remove the brisket and keep it on the side

4. Add onion and Saute
5. Add curry powder, seared beef, fish sauce, ginger, diced tomatoes, star anise
6. Pour the apple sauce and stir well
7. Add bay leaf and lemon grass
8. Pour broth and lock up the lid
9. Cook on HIGH pressure for 35 minutes and release the pressure naturally
10. Add carrots and lock up the lid again, cook on HIGH pressure for 7 minutes
11. Release the pressure naturally and serve!

Nutrition Values (Per Serving)

- Calories: 462
- Fats: 20g
- Carbs:15g
- Fiber:2g

Beef Stroganoff

Serves 4

Prep Time: 10 minutes

Cook Time: 15 minutes

Ingredients

- 2 cups of beef strip
- 3 tablespoon of olive oil
- 1 tablespoon of almond flour
- 1 chopped up onion
- 2 minced up garlic cloves
- 1 cup of sliced mushroom
- 2 tablespoon of tomato paste
- 3 tablespoon of Worcestershire sauce
- 2 cups of beef broth
- 1 and a ½ cup of zucchini zoodles
- ¼ teaspoon of salt
- ¼ teaspoon of pepper

Directions

1. Take a taking a bowl and add in the salt, pepper and flour alongside the beef strips
2. Coat up the beef with the flour and the seasoning
3. Set your instant pot on low heat and low pressure and place your meat in your inner pot and cook for 10 minutes

4. *Add in the rest of your ingredients in your pot Close up the lid and let it cook for about 18 minutes at medium pressure*
5. *Once done, release the pressure naturally*
6. *Serve finally alongside a good bunch of zoodles*

Nutrition Values (Per Serving)

- Calories: 335
- Fat: 18g
- Carbohydrates: 22g
- Protein: 20.02g

Exquisite Thai Brisket

Serves 9

Prep Time: 10 minutes

Cook Time: 35 minutes

Ingredients

- 3 pound of grass fed beef brisket
- 2 teaspoon of kosher salt
- 1 tablespoon of Thai curry paste
- 1 and a ½ cup of full fat coconut milk (additional ½ a cup)
- 2 tablespoon of coconut aminos
- 2 tablespoon of apple juice (won't cause trouble in such small amount)
- 1 tablespoon of Red Boat Fish Sauce
- 2 medium sized sweet potatoes
- 2 small sized peeled and coarsely chopped onion
- 2 large sized peeled carrots cut up into 2 inch pieces
- Just a handful of mixed herbs (cilantro and scallions)

Directions

1. *Take a large sized bowl and add the cubed up beef*
2. *Season them with salt*
3. *Add curry paste and give it a nice stir*

4. Pour coconut milk, apple juice, coconut aminos, fish sauce and stir well

5. Add onion, potatoes, beef cubes and carrots and give it a nice stir

6. Lock up the lid and set your pot t o MEAT mode

7. Cook for 35 minutes

8. Release the pressure naturally and transfer the meat to a serving platter

9. Pour the veggies and sauce to a blender alongside ½ a cup of coconut milk

10. Puree and pour the sauce over the beef

11. Enjoy!

Nutrition Values (Per Serving)

- Calories: 362
- Fat: 24g
- Carbohydrates: 27g
- Protein: 14g

Fancy Mexican Meatloaf

Serves 4

Prep Time: 5 minutes

Cook Time: 25 minutes

Ingredients

- 2 pound of ground organic beef
- 1 cup of roasted salsa
- 1 teaspoon of cumin
- 1 teaspoon of chili powder
- 1 teaspoon of garlic
- 1 teaspoon of paprika
- 1 teaspoon of onion powder
- 1 teaspoon of sea salt
- 1 teaspoon of ground black pepper
- 1 diced onion
- 1 pastured egg
- ¼ cup of tapioca start
- 1 tablespoon of ghee

Directions

1. *Take a bowl and mix all of the ingredients*
2. *Take a meat loaf pan and transfer the mixture to the pan*
3. *Set your pot to Saute mode and add a teaspoon of ghee, allow the ghee to heat up*
4. *Add meatloaf to the pot and lock up the lid*

5. Cook for about 35 minutes on MEAT/STEW settings
6. Release the pressure naturally
7. Serve with a sprinkle of cilantro
8. Enjoy!

Nutrition Values (Per Serving)

- Calories: 170
- Fats: 5g
- Carbs:9g
- Fiber:3g

Original Texan Beef Chili

Serves 4

Prep Time: 10 minutes

Cook Time: 35 minutes

Ingredients

- 1 pound of grass fed organic feed
- 1 sliced and seeded green bell pepper
- 1 large sized onion
- 4 large pieces of chopped up small carrot
- ½ a teaspoon of ground black pepper
- 1 teaspoon of sea salt
- 1 teaspoon of onion powder
- 1 tablespoon of chopped up fresh parsley
- 1 tablespoon of Worcestershire sauce
- 4 teaspoon of chili powder
- 1 teaspoon of paprika
- 1 teaspoon of garlic powder
- Just a pinch of cumin

Directions

1. Set your pot to Saute mode and add ground beef, Saute it until nicely browned
2. Add the remaining ingredients and stir it
3. Lock up the lid and cook on MEAT/STEW mode for 35 minutes

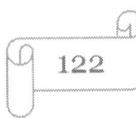

4. *Release the pressure naturally over 10 minutes*

5. *Open the lid and enjoy*

Nutrition Values (Per Serving)

- Calories: 220
- Fats: 10g
- Carbs:21g
- Fiber:5g

Fantastic Beef and Potato Casserole

<u>Serves</u> 3

<u>Prep Time:</u> 10 minutes

<u>Cook Time:</u> 15 minutes

Ingredients

- 1 pound of ground beef
- 2 cups of cubed up potatoes
- 2 cups of tomato sauce
- 2 cups of beef broth
- 2 tablespoon of butter
- 1 chopped up yellow onion
- 5 pieces of broccoli florets
- 1 cup of Whole30 Mayonnaise

Directions

1. *Set your pot to Saute mode and add butter, allow the butter to melt*
2. *Add onion and caramelize it for a few minutes*
3. *Add beef and lock up the lid*
4. *Cook on HIGH pressure for 5 minutes*
5. *Release the pressure naturally and give it a nice stir*
6. *Add potatoes, broccoli and beef broth*
7. *Lock up the lid and cook on LOW pressure for 5 minutes*
8. *Release the pressure naturally and stir n spices and tomato sauce*

9. *Top it up with mayo and enjoy!*

Nutritional Values (Per Serving)

- Calories: 144
- Fat: 6.8g
- Carbohydrates: 2.1g
- Protein: 18g

Mexicana Carne Guisana

<u>Serves</u> 4

<u>Prep Time:</u> 10 minutes

<u>Cook Time:</u> 40 minutes

Ingredients

- 2 tablespoon of avocado oil
- 1 pound of beef stew meat
- 1 diced onion
- 1 tablespoon of minced garlic
- 1 Serrano pepper , minced up
- 1 piece of bay leaf
- 1 teaspoon of ground cumin
- 1 teaspoon of chili powder
- 1 teaspoon of paprika
- 1 teaspoon of salt
- ½ teaspoon of pepper
- ½ teaspoon of oregano
- ½ a cup of tomato sauce
- 1 tablespoon of potato starch

Directions

1. Set your pot to Saute mode and add oil
2. Allow the oil to heat up and add beef cubes
3. Sear all sides until browned

4. Once the meat is browned, add onion, bay leaf, garlic, spice, Serrano pepper

5. Stir fry everything for 2-3 minutes

6. Pour beef broth, tomato sauce and lock up the lid

7. Cook on MEAT/STEW mode for 35 minutes

8. Once done, release the pressure naturally

9. Unlock the lid and remove it

10. Take a bowl and add potato flour ,starch and stir well to make a slurry

11. Add the slurry to the pot and stir well

12. Serve it over cauliflower rice

13. Enjoy!

Nutrition Values (Per Serving)

- Calories: 454
- Fat: 14g
- Carbohydrates: 577g
- Protein: 35g

Chapter 7: Lamb Recipes

Generously Prepared Lamb Spare Ribs

<u>Serves</u> 5

<u>Prep Time:</u> 4-5 hours

<u>Cook Time:</u> 20 minutes

Ingredients

Ingredients for the Lamb

- 2.5 pounds of pastured lamb spare ribs
- 2 teaspoons of kosher salt
- 1 tablespoon of curry powder

Ingredients for the sauce

- 1 t tablespoon of coconut oil
- 1 large sized coarsely chopped onion
- ½ a pound of minced garlic
- 1 tablespoon of curry powder
- 1 tablespoon of kosher salt
- Juice from about 1 lemon
- 1 and a 1/4th cup of divided cilantro
- 4 thinly sliced scallion

Directions

1. Take a bowl and add your spare ribs

2. Season them with 2 teaspoon of salt, 1 teaspoon of curry powder and mix well and coat the ribs fully

3. Cover them up and allow to chill for 4 hours

4. Set your pot to Saute mode and add coconut oil, allow the oil to heat up

5. Add the spare ribs and brown them

6. Transfer to another plate

7. Take a blender and add tomato, onion and blend to a paste

8. Add minced garlic to your pot (while in Saute mode) and keep stirring while adding the paste

9. Add curry powder, chopped cilantro, lemon juice and salt

10. Allow the mixture to reach a boil and stir n the ribs

11. Lock up the lid and cook for 20 minutes at HIGH pressure

12. Allow the pressure to release naturally once done

13. Scoop out the grease and season with some salt

14. Enjoy!

Nutrition Values (Per Serving)

- Calories: 165
- Fats: 14g
- Carbs:5g
- Fiber:2g

Inspiring Lamb Stew

<u>Serves</u> 6

<u>Prep Time:</u> 5 minutes

<u>Cook Time:</u> 40 minutes

Ingredients

- 2 pound of lamb stew meat cut up into 1 inch cubes
- 1 acorn squash
- 3 large pieces of carrots
- 1 large sized yellow onion
- 2 sprigs of rosemary
- 1 bay leaf
- 6 cloves of sliced garlic
- 3 tablespoon of broth
- ¼-1/2 a teaspoon of salt

Directions

1. *Peel the squash and deseed them*
2. *Cube the squash*
3. *Slice up the carrots into circles*
4. *Peel the onion in half and slice the halves into half moons*
5. *Add all of the ingredients (including veggies) to your pot and lock up the lid*
6. *Cook on HIGH pressure for 25 minutes*
7. *Release the pressure naturally and serve!*

Nutrition Values (Per Serving)

- Calories: 271
- Fat: 20g
- Carbohydrates: 5g
- Protein: 13g

The Proper Fan Favorite Lamb Shanks

<u>Serves</u> 5

<u>Prep Time:</u> 10 minutes

<u>Cook Time:</u> 45 minutes

Ingredients

- 3 pound of lamb shanks
- Amount of Kosher Salt
- Freshly ground portions of black pepper
- 2 tablespoon of well divided ghee
- 2 roughly chopped up medium sized carrots
- 2 celery roughly chopped up celery stalks
- 1 roughly chopped up large sized onion
- 1 tablespoon of tomato paste
- 3 cloves of peeled and smashed garlic
- 1 cup of bone broth
- 1 teaspoon of Red Boast Fish Sauce
- 1 tablespoon of vinegar

Directions

1. Season the shanks properly with salt and pepper
2. Melt a teaspoon of ghee in your Pot (Setting it to Saute mode) and add the shanks
3. Cook for about 8-10 minutes until a nice brown texture appears
4. Chop the vegetables

5. Once the lamb is ready, remove it from the pot
6. Add the veggies and season with some salt and pepper
7. Add a tablespoon of ghee as well
8. Once the veggies are ready, pour garlic clove, tomato paste and stir well for a minute
9. Add shanks to the veggie mix
10. Add tomatoes
11. Pour bone broth, vinegar and fish sauce
12. Sprinkle pepper and lock up the lid
13. Once the pressure is high, cook for 45 minutes
14. Once done, release the pressure naturally
15. Serve shanks and enjoy!

Nutrition Values (Per Serving)

- Calories: 377
- Fats: 16g
- Carbs: 10g
- Fiber: 2g

The Great Indian Lamb

<u>Serves</u> 4

<u>Prep Time:</u> 10 minutes

<u>Cook Time:</u> 45 minutes

Ingredients

- 2 tablespoon of avocado oil
- 2 pound of lamb meat
- 2 diced onion
- 1 and a ½ inch knob of fresh ginger minced up
- 3 minced cloves of garlic
- 1 bay leaf
- 4 whole cloves
- 4 cardamom pods
- 1 tablespoon of coriander powder
- 1 teaspoon of cumin powder
- 2 teaspoon of salt
- 1 teaspoon of turmeric powder
- 1 teaspoon of Kashmiri chili powder
- 1 teaspoon of paprika
- 2 cans of organic diced tomatoes
- 1 teaspoon of Garam masala
- ½ a cup of water
- ½ a pound of potatoes cut up in half

Directions

1. Set your pot to Saute mode and add oil, allow the oil to heat up
2. Add the meat and brown it
3. Once the meat starts to brown, add onion, garlic, ginger, spices, bay leaf and stir fry for 2-3 minutes
4. Pour water and diced tomatoes
5. Lock up the lid and cook on MEAT/STEW settings for 45 minutes
6. Release the pressure naturally and set your pot to Saute mode
7. Allow the stew to warm up for a while until you have a thick soup
8. Enjoy!

Nutrition Values (Per Serving)

- Calories: 559
- Fat: 29g
- Carbohydrates: 18g
- Protein: 57g

Very Indian Middle "Eastern" Lamb Stew

<u>Serves</u> 4

<u>Prep Time:</u> 15 minutes

<u>Cook Time:</u> 75 minutes

Ingredients

- 2 tablespoon of ghee
- 1 and a ½ pound of lamb stew meat, cut up into 1 and a ½ inch cubes
- 1 diced up onion
- 4-6 cloves of roughly chopped garlic
- Teaspoon of salt
- 1 teaspoon of pepper
- 1 teaspoon of cumin
- 1 teaspoon of coriander
- 1 teaspoon of turmeric
- 1 teaspoon of cinnamon
- 1 teaspoon of cumin seeds
- ½ a teaspoon of chili flakes
- 2 tablespoon of tomato paste
- ¼ cup of apple cider vinegar
- 1 and a ¼ cup of chicken stock
- ¼ cup of dried chopped apricots
- 2 tablespoon of date paste

Directions

1. Set your pot to Saute mode and add ghee, allow it to heat up
2. Add onion and Saute for 3-4 minutes until a nice fragrance comes
3. Add lamb, salt, garlic and spices and Saute them for 5 minutes until they release a nice fragrance
4. Add vinegar, date paste, tomato paste, stock and apricots and stir well
5. Lock up the lid and cook on HIGH pressure for 60 minutes
6. Release the pressure naturally
7. Serve with a garnish of fresh cilantro
8. Enjoy!

Nutrition Values (Per Serving)

- Calories: 563
- Fat: 22g
- Carbohydrates: 41g
- Protein: 49g

The Mediterranean Leg Lamb Roast!

<u>Serves</u> 4

<u>Prep Time:</u> 15 minutes

<u>Cook Time:</u> 75 minutes

Ingredients

- 2 tablespoon of olive oil
- 5-6 pound of lamb leg (boneless)
- 1 teaspoon of sea salt
- 1 crushed bay leaf
- ½ a teaspoon of pepper
- 1 teaspoon of marjoram
- 1 teaspoon of sage
- 3 cloves of minced garlic
- 1 teaspoon of ginger
- 1 teaspoon of thyme
- 2 cups of broth
- 2 and a ½ pound of potatoes peeled up and cut into 2-3 inch pieces
- A mixture of 2-3 tablespoon of arrowroot powder and 1/3 cup of water

Directions

1. *Set your pot to Saute mode and add olive oil*

2. Add the roast and swirl it around to ensure that it is coated with the oil
3. Sear on one side and flip over, sear the other side
4. Sprinkle salt, pepper and herbs
5. Add broth
6. Lock up the lid and cook on HIGH pressure for 50 minutes
7. Release the pressure quickly
8. Check if the potatoes are cooked well
9. Take a slotted spoon and transfer the potatoes alongside the roast to a serving platter
10. Cover and keep them warm
11. Whisk in the prepared arrowroot mixture into the pot and wait until thick (keep the pot in Saute mode during this step)
12. Pour the sauce over the roast and enjoy!

Nutrition Values (Per Serving)

- Calories: 487
- Fat: 45g
- Carbohydrates: 0g
- Protein: 19g

Authentic Moroccan Lamb Stew

Prep Time: 10 minutes

Cook Time: 40 minutes

Ingredients

- 1 pound of lamb stew meat
- 2 cups of chopped up carrots
- 2 cups of chopped up sweet potatoes
- 1 medium sized white onion
- 3 cups of chopped kale
- 23 cloves of chopped garlic
- ¼ cup of finely chopped dried apricots
- 2 cans of diced tomatoes
- 2 and a ½ cup of chicken broth
- 3 tablespoon of coconut aminos
- Olive oil as needed

For Spices

- 1 teaspoon of salt
- Black pepper as needed
- ½ a teaspoon of ground ginger
- 1 teaspoon of ground cumin
- 1 teaspoon of cinnamon
- ¼ teaspoon of curry powder
- ¼ teaspoon of ground turmeric

- ¼ teaspoon of allspice

Directions

1. *Chop up the lamb into small pieces*
2. *Set your pot to Saute mode and add meat*
3. *Drizzle a bit of olive oil*
4. *Saute the meat until browned and add the stew ingredients*
5. *Lock up the lid and cook on HIGH pressure for 20 minutes*
6. *Release the pressure naturally*
7. *Serve over some cauliflower rice*
8. *Enjoy!*

Nutrition Values (Per Serving)

- Calories: 306
- Fat: 20g
- Carbohydrates: 26g
- Protein: 5g

Very "Instant" Lamb Rogan Josh

<u>Serves</u> 4

<u>Prep Time:</u> 10 minutes

<u>Cook Time:</u> 40 minutes

Ingredients

- 1 pound of lamb deboned and cut up into 1 and a ½ inch cubes
- 4 tablespoon of coconut cream
- ½ a teaspoon of Garam Masala

For Spices

- 1 tablespoon of olive oil
- 2 pieces of bay leaves
- 3 pieces of cracked open cardamom pods
- 2 pieces of whole cloves
- 1 and a ½ teaspoon of cumin seeds
- 1 and a ½ teaspoon of fennel seeds
- 2 cloves of minced garlic
- ½ a teaspoon of Garam Masala
- ½ a teaspoon of ground chili
- 1 teaspoon of ground coriander
- 1 teaspoon of ground cumin
- 1 teaspoon ground ginger
- 2 finely diced tomatoes

- 1 tablespoon of fresh coriander
- Sea salt as needed

Directions

1. *Make the marinade by mixing coconut cream and Garam Masala together*
2. *Rub it all over the lamb and allow it to chill for 24 hours*
3. *Set your pot to Saute mode and add oil, whole spices and sizzle them briefly until aroma is released*
4. *Add garlic and stir well*
5. *Add the rest of the powdered spices and cook for a while, add fresh tomatoes, water and tomato puree*
6. *Add the marinated lamb and give it a nice stir*
7. *Cancel the Saute mode and lock up the lid*
8. *Cook on HIGH pressure for 10 minutes*
9. *Do a quick release*
10. *Remove the lid and set the pot to Saute mode*
11. *Stir well for a few minutes and check the seasoning*
12. *Serve over some cauliflower rice and enjoy!*

Nutrition Values (Per Serving)

- Calories: 563
- Fat: 22g
- Carbohydrates: 41g
- Protein: 49g

Simple Boneless Lamb Leg

<u>Serves</u> 8-10

<u>Prep Time:</u> 5 minutes

<u>Cook Time:</u> 35 minutes

Ingredients

- 3-4 pound of boneless leg lamb
- Salt as needed
- Pepper as needed
- 2 tablespoon of avocado oil
- 2 cups of water
- 4 cloves of crushed garlic
- 2 tablespoon of chopped up fresh rosemary

Directions

1. *Pat the lamb dry using a kitchen towel*
2. *Season with pepper and salt*
3. *Set the pot to Saute mode and add oil*
4. *Once the oil is hot, add the lamb and brown them*
5. *Remove the lamb rub the lamb's upper and side with rosemary and garlic*
6. *Place a steamer rack on the pot*
7. *Pour water to the pot*
8. *Place the lamb on the rack and lock up the lid*
9. *Cook on HIGH pressure for 30 minutes*
10. *Allow the pressure to release naturally and remove the lid*

11. Pre-heat and prepare your broiler and transfer the roast to a broiler pan

12. Place it about 6 inch away from the heat source and broil for 2 minutes

13. Remove and allow it to rest

14. Slice it up and enjoy!

Nutrition Values (Per Serving)

- Calories: 432
- Fat: 25g
- Carbohydrates: 1g
- Protein: 44g

Chapter 8: Vegetarian Recipes

The Perfect Mashed Cauliflower and Potato Medley

<u>Serves</u> 4

<u>Prep Time:</u> 5 minutes

<u>Cook Time:</u> 15 minutes

Ingredients

- 1 and a ½ cups of water
- 2 pound of potatoes sliced up into 1 inch pieces
- 8 ounce of cauliflower florets
- ½ a teaspoon of salt
- 1 minced garlic clove

Directions

1. Add water to your Instant Pot and add the florets
2. Add the potatoes
3. Lock up the lid and cook on HIGH pressure for 5 minutes
4. Release the pressure naturally
5. Sprinkle a bit of salt and add a piece of garlic, mash the whole mixture well
6. Serve!

Nutrition Values (Per Serving)

- Calories: 249
- Fat: 0.6g
- Carbohydrates: 55g
- Protein: 7.5g

Lovely Cauliflower Rice

<u>Serves</u> 4

<u>Prep Time:</u> 5 minutes

<u>Cook Time:</u> 15 minutes

Ingredients

- 1 large sized cauliflower head
- 2 tablespoon of olive oil
- ¼ teaspoon of salt
- ½ a teaspoon of dried parsley
- ¼ teaspoon of cumin
- ¼ teaspoon of turmeric
- ¼ teaspoon of paprika
- Fresh cilantro
- Lime wedges

Directions

1. Wash the cauliflower well and trim the leaves
2. Place a steamer rack on top of the pot and transfer the florets to the rack
3. Add 1 cup of water into the pot
4. Lock up the lid and cook on HIGH pressure for 1 minutes
5. Once done, do a quick release
6. Transfer the flower to a serving platter
7. Set your pot to Saute mode and add oil, allow the oil tot heat up

8. Add flowers back to the pot and cook,, making sure to break them using potato masher
9. Add spices and season with a bit of salt
10. Give a nice stir and squeeze a bit of lime
11. Serve and enjoy!

Nutrition Values (Per Serving)

- Calories: 169
- Fat: 14g
- Carbohydrates: 10g
- Protein: 3g

Sweet Butternut Squash Soup

<u>Serves</u> 4

<u>Prep Time:</u> 5 minutes

<u>Cook Time:</u> 30 minutes

Ingredients

For Soup

- 1 teaspoon of extra virgin olive oil
- 1 large sized chopped up onion
- 2 minced garlic cloves
- 1 tablespoon of curry powder
- 3 pound of butternut squash, cut up into 1 inch cubes and peeled
- 3 cups of water
- ½ a cup of coconut milk

For Extra Toppings

- Hulled up pumpkin seeds
- Dried up cranberries

Directions

1. *Set your pot to Saute mode and add olive oil, allow the oil to heat up*
2. *Add onions and Saute for 8 minutes*
3. *Add garlic, curry powder and Saute for 1 minute*

4. *Cancel Saute mode and add butternut squash, water and salt*
5. *Lock up the lid and cook on HIGH pressure for 30 minutes*
6. *Naturally release the pressure once done*
7. *Open the lid and puree using an immersion blender*
8. *Stir in coconut milk and season with a bit of salt*
9. *Serve with a topping of dried cranberries and enjoy!*

Nutrition Values (Per Serving)

- Calories: 124
- Fat: 6g
- Carbohydrates: 18g
- Protein: 2g

Healthy Beet Mix

<u>Serves</u> 6

<u>Prep Time:</u> 5 minutes

<u>Cook Time:</u> 15 minutes

Ingredients

- 6 medium sized beets
- 1 cup of water
- Kosher salt
- Freshly ground black pepper
- Balsamic vinegar
- Extra virgin olive oil

Directions

1. Wash the beets carefully and trim them to ½ inch portions

2. Add 1 cup of water to the pot

3. Place a steamer/ trivet on top and arrange the beets on top of the steamer

4. Lock up the lid and cook on HIGH pressure for 1 minute

5. Release the pressure naturally and allow the beet to cool

6. Slice the top of the skin carefully

7. Slice up the beets in uniform portions and season with salt and pepper

8. Add a splash of balsamic vinegar and allow them to marinate for 30 minutes

9. Add a bit of extra olive oil and serve!

Nutrition Values (Per Serving)

- Calories: 24
- Fat: 0g
- Carbohydrates: 5g
- Protein: 1g

Fantastic Guacamole Spread

<u>Serves</u> 6

<u>Prep Time:</u> 5 minutes

<u>Cook Time:</u> 5 minutes

Ingredients

- 1 large sized avocado
- ¼ finely chopped red onion
- ½ of a juice lime
- 1 finely chopped sprig cilantro
- 1 pinch of salt

Directions

1. Halve your avocados vertically and remove the pit
2. Run a knife vertically through the flesh followed by horizontal slices
3. Take a spoon and scoop out cubed avocado pieces from the skin
4. Transfer them to a bowl
5. Mash the avocado and mix in lime juice, salt, onion, cilantro
6. Serve as a spread!

Nutrition Values (Per Serving)

- Calories: 50
- Fat: 4.4g

- Carbohydrates: 3.1g
- Protein: 0.7g

The Definitive Brussels

<u>Serves</u> 4

<u>Prep Time:</u> 5 minutes

<u>Cook Time:</u> 5 minutes

Ingredients

- 2 pound of halved Brussels sprouts
- ¼ cup of coconut aminos
- 2 tablespoon of sriracha sauce
- 1 tablespoon of vinegar
- 2 tablespoon of sesame oil (Allow in Whole30 when used in small amounts)
- 1 tablespoon of chopped almonds
- 1 teaspoon of red pepper flakes
- 2 teaspoon of garlic powder
- 1 teaspoon of onion powder
- 1 tablespoon of smoked paprika
- ½ a tablespoon of cayenne pepper
- Salt as needed
- Pepper as needed

Directions

1. Set your pot to Saute mode and add almonds
2. Saute for a while
3. Take a bowl and add the remaining ingredients (excluding the Brussels) and mix well

4. Add the Brussels to the pot

5. Add the prepared mixture to the pot

6. Stir and lock up the lid

7. Cook on HIGH pressure for 3 minutes

8. Release the pressure naturally and serve

9. Enjoy!

Nutrition Values (Per Serving)

- Calories: 84
- Fat: 7g
- Carbohydrates: 5g
- Protein: 2g

Tenderly Roasted Potatoes

<u>Serves</u> 8

<u>Prep Time:</u> 5 minutes

<u>Cook Time:</u> 7 minutes

Ingredients

- ¼ cup of avocado oil
- 1 and a ½ pound of russet potatoes
- ½ a teaspoon of onion powder
- 1 teaspoon of garlic powder
- 1 teaspoon of sea salt
- ¼ teaspoon of paprika
- ¼ teaspoon of ground black pepper
- 1 cup of chicken broth

Directions

1. Slice the potato into wedge shapes

2. Set the pot to Saute mode and add your fat, allow the fat to heat up and melt

3. Once the fat is hot, add potatoes to the pot and roast for 5-8 minutes

4. Give it a nice stir

5. Sprinkle a bit of seasoning and add the broth

6. Cancel the Saute mode and lock up the lid

7. Cook on HIGH pressure for about 7 minutes

8. Do a quick release

9. Open the lid and season with a bit of salt

10. Enjoy!

Nutrition Values (Per Serving)

- Calories: 111
- Fat: 2g
- Carbohydrates: 22g
- Protein: 3g

Elegant Carrot Soup

<u>Serves</u> 2

<u>Prep Time:</u> 15 minutes

<u>Cook Time:</u> 10 minutes

Ingredients

- 5 medium sized chopped and peeled potatoes
- 8 peeled and chopped carrots
- ½ of a chopped yellow onion
- 3 minced garlic cloves
- 2 cups of finely chopped fresh kale
- 1 tablespoon of curry powder
- 1 teaspoon of cayenne pepper
- 4 cups of water
- 2 cups of vegetable broth

Directions

1. Mince up the garlic and chop onions

2. Add them to your pot and alongside ¼ cup of water and Saute for minutes

3. Add cayenne, vegetable broth, curry powder, broth and stir well

4. Add water and Saute for 2 minutes more

5. Add the rest of the ingredients (except kale) and lock up the lid

6. Cook on HIGH pressure for 8 minutes

7. Release the pressure naturally
8. Use an immersion blender and blender well until you have a soup like texture
9. Chop up the kale and stir in
10. Serve and enjoy!

Nutrition Values (Per Serving)

- Calories: 155
- Fat: 11g
- Carbohydrates: 16g
- Protein: 2g

The Good Old Baked Potato

<u>Serves</u> 4

<u>Prep Time:</u> 5 minutes

<u>Cook Time:</u> 20 minutes

Ingredients

- 1 cup of water
- 2 pound of medium baking potatoes (finely washed and scrubbed)

Directions

1. Wash the potatoes carefully and add them to your pot

2. Make sure to pierce the sides of the potatoes thoroughly using a fork

3. Add a cup of water

4. Pre-heat your oven to 450 degree Fahrenheit

5. Lock up the lid and cook the potatoes for 10 minutes over HIGH pressure

6. Allow the pressure to release naturally over 10 minutes

7. Take tongs and take the small potatoes out and transfer them to the middle rack of your oven, bake for 10-15 minutes (turn the heat off)

8. Repeat with the large potatoes for 10 minutes (do not turn heat on again)

9. Enjoy!

Nutrition Values (Per Serving)

- Calories: 150
- Fat: 0g
- Carbohydrates: 39g
- Protein: 6g

Friendly Spaghetti Squash with Sage and Garlic

<u>Serves</u> 4

<u>Prep Time:</u> 5 minutes

<u>Cook Time:</u> 15 minutes

Ingredients

- 1 medium sized spaghetti squash
- 1 cup of water
- 1 small bunch of fresh sage
- 3-5 cloves of sliced garlic
- 2 tablespoon of olive oil
- 1 teaspoon of salt
- 1/8 teaspoon of nutmeg

Directions

1. Halve your squash and scoop out any seed

2. Add water to the pot and place a trivet on top

3. Place the squash on the trivet making sure that the flesh side is facing up

4. Make sure to stack them up one on top the other

5. Lock up the lid and cook on HIGH pressure for 3-4 minutes

6. Take a pan and place it over low heat

7. Add sage and garlic with a bit of olive oil and Saute them

8. Once the cooking is done, allow the pressure to release naturally

9. *Take the squash out tear out the flesh using a fork and transfer them into the pan*

10. *Once all of the squash has been transferred, turn down the heat and sprinkle a bit of salt and nutmeg*

11. *Mix and enjoy!*

Nutrition Values (Per Serving)

- Calories: 88
- Fat: 4g
- Carbohydrates: 13g
- Protein: 1.5g

Slightly "Stinky" Onion Soup

<u>Serves</u> 6

<u>Prep Time:</u> 5 minutes

<u>Cook Time:</u> 25 minutes

Ingredients

- 2 tablespoon of avocado oil
- 8 cups of yellow onion
- 1 tablespoon of balsamic vinegar
- 6 cups of pork stock
- 1 teaspoon of salt
- 2 bay leaves
- 2 large sprigs

Directions

1. Set your pot to Saute mode and add the onions (sliced up in half-moon shapes)
2. Cook them for about 15 minutes
3. Add a bit of balsamic vinegar and scrape the bottom
4. Add stock, thyme, bay leaves and salt
5. Lock up the lid and cook on HIGH pressure for 10 minutes
6. Release the pressure naturally over 10 minutes
7. Discard the bay leaves and thyme stems
8. Take an immersion blender and blend the whole mixture
9. Transfer it to a bowl and enjoy!

Nutrition Values (Per Serving)

- Calories: 219
- Fat: 7g
- Carbohydrates: 32g
- Protein: 9g

Coming Age Pumpkin Soup

Serves: 4

Prep Time:5 minutes

Cook Time: 15 minutes

Ingredients

- 1 piece of chopped onion
- 2 tablespoon of clarified butter
- 3 tablespoon of almond flour
- 2 tablespoon of curry powder
- 4 cups of low sodium vegetable broth
- 1 cup of water
- 4 cups of fresh pumpkin puree
- 1 and a ½ cups of fat free half and half
- 2 tablespoon of coconut aminos
- 1 teaspoon of lemon juice
- Just a pinch cayenne pepper
- Salt as needed
- Pepper as needed

Directions

1. Grease your pot with olive oil and set your pot to Saute mode
2. Add onion and cook them for a few minutes
3. Add clarified butter and allow the butter to heat up
4. Add flour, curry powder and stir until smooth

5. Once it begins to bubble, add water and broth

6. Stir in pumpkin, chopped up onion, aminos, pepper and salt

7. Cook for 3 minutes at HIGH pressure

8. Quick release the pressure and remove the lid

9. Set your cooker to Saute mode again and stir in fat free half and half

10. Blend the soup using an immersion blender and bring the soup to a boil

11. Turn the heat off and stir in a bit of lemon juice

12. Enjoy!

Nutritional Values (Per Serving)

- Calories : 41
- Fat : 4g
- Carbohydrates : 1g
- Protein : 1g

Aromatic Garlic Potato

<u>Serves</u> 4

<u>Prep Time:</u> 5 minutes

<u>Cook Time:</u> 5 minutes

Ingredients

- 4 medium sized russet yellow potatoes
- 1 cup of vegetable broth
- 6 cloves of garlic, peeled up and cut up into half
- ½ a cup of almond milk
- Salt as needed
- ¼ cup of chopped parsley

Directions

1. Cut the potatoes into 8-12 chunks

2. Add them to your pot

3. Add broth and garlic

4. Lock up the lid and cook under HIGH pressure for 4 minutes

5. Release the pressure naturally

6. Mash the potatoes using a masher and add a bit of almond milk if needed

7. Stir well and serve hot!

Nutrition Values (Per Serving)

- Calories: 293
- Fat: 14g
- Carbohydrates: 35g
- Protein: 8g

Everybody's Most Wanted Pickled Green Chilies

<u>Serves</u> 1 and ½ cups

<u>Prep Time:</u> 10 minutes

<u>Cook Time:</u> 11 minutes

Ingredients

- 1 pound of green chilies
- 1 and a ½ cups of apple cider vinegar
- 1 teaspoon of pickling salt
- 1 and a ½ teaspoon of date paste
- ¼ teaspoon of garlic powder

Directions

1. Add the above mentioned ingredients to the pot

2. Lock up the lid and cook on HIGH pressure for 10 minutes

3. Release the pressure naturally

4. Spoon the mix into washed jars and cover the slices with a bit of cooking liquid

5. Add vinegar to submerge the chilly

6. Enjoy!

Nutrition Values (Per Serving)

- Calories: 3.1
- Fat: 0g
- Carbohydrates: 0.6g

- Protein: 0.1g

Subtle Zucchini Pesto Pasta

Prep Time: 3 minutes

Cook Time: 10 minutes

Ingredients

- 1 tablespoon of olive oil
- 1 roughly chopped up onion
- 2 and a ½ pound of roughly chopped zucchini
- ½ a cup of water
- 1 and a ½ teaspoon of salt
- 1 bunch of basil leaves (picked off)
- 2 roughly minced garlic clove
- 1 tablespoon of extra virgin olive oil
- Extra zucchini for making Zoodles

Directions

1. Set the pot to Saute mode and add olive oil

2. Allow the oil to heat up

3. Add onion and Saute f or 4 minutes

4. Add zucchini, salt and water

5. Lock up the lid and cook on HIGH pressure for 3 minutes

6. Release the pressure naturally

7. Add basil leaves and garlic

8. Use an immersion blender to blend until you have a sauce like consistency

9. Take extra zucchini and pass them through Spiralizer to obtain noodle like shapes
10. Toss the Zoodles with the sauce and enjoy!

Nutrition Values (Per Serving)

- Calories: 71
- Fat: 4.7g
- Carbohydrates: 7.5g
- Protein: 1.2g

Energizing Celery Soup

<u>Serves</u> 3

<u>Prep Time:</u> 10 minutes

<u>Cook Time:</u> 30 minutes

Ingredients

- 1 large sized celery root chopped up into 4-5 cups
- 1 medium sized chopped onion
- 4 peeled garlic cloves
- 3 cups of vegetable broth (divided)
- 1/8 teaspoon of white pepper
- ½ a teaspoon of thyme
- ½ a teaspoon of salt
- ¼ cup of almond milk
- ½ a teaspoon of lemon juice

Directions

1. Peel the celery root and cut them up into equal sized cubes
2. Set the pot to Saute mode and add onion and garlic
3. Brown them
4. Add celery roots and 2 cups of broth
5. Lock up the lid and cook on HIGH pressure for 4 minutes
6. Allow the pressure to release naturally
7. Pour cooked celery and broth into the blender

8. Blend the mixture well until you have a smooth consistency, start from low and go to high
9. Transfer it to back to the pot
10. Add white pepper, thyme and salt
11. Set the pot to Saute mode and simmer for 20 minutes
12. Add almond milk and lemon juice
13. Keep stirring for 5 minutes
14. Add a bit of pepper and salt
15. Enjoy!

Nutrition Value (Per Serving)

- Calories: 214
- Fat: 13g
- Carbohydrates: 20g
- Protein: 6g

Simply "Squash" Spaghetti As You Like It

<u>Serves</u> 4

<u>Prep Time:</u> 5 minutes

<u>Cook Time:</u> 7 minutes

Ingredients

- 2 pound of spaghetti squash
- 1 cup of water

Directions

1. *Take a pairing knife and cut up the spaghetti squash in half*
2. *Take a large sized spoon and scoop out the seeds and discard the gunk*
3. *Place a steamer rack and place it over your pot*
4. *Transfer the squash to the rack and add 1 cup of water to the pot*
5. *Make sure that the cut part of the halved squash are facing up*
6. *Lock up the lid and cook on HIGH pressure for 7 minutes*
7. *Quick release the pressure*
8. *Take the squash out and add a bit of sauce and your favorite topping*
9. *Enjoy the Squash noodles!*

Nutrition Value (Per Serving)

- Calories: 45

- Fats: 5g
- Carbs: 7g
- Fiber: 3g

Broccoli and Apple Soup

<u>Serves</u> 4

<u>Prep Time:</u> 5 minutes

<u>Cook Time:</u> 5 minutes

Ingredients

- 2 tablespoon of olive oil
- The white parts of 3 medium sized leeks
- 2 roughly chopped medium sized shallots
- 1 tablespoon of Indian curry powder
- Kosher salt
- 1 and a 12 pound of chopped up broccoli
- ¼ cup of peeled up and diced apple
- 4 cups of vegetable broth
- Freshly ground black pepper
- 1 cup of full fat coconut milk

Directions

1. Set the pot to Saute mode and add oil, allow the oil to heat up
2. Add vegetables and Saute them
3. Add curry powder and sprinkle a bit of salt
4. Stir well until a nice aroma comes out
5. Add chopped up apple and broccoli and stir well
6. Pour vegetable broth and submerge the veggies
7. Lock up the lid and cook on HIGH pressure for 5 minutes
8. Release the pressure naturally

9. Take an immersion blender and blend the mixture well until you have a nice soup like consistency

10. Pour coconut milk and season with a bit of salt and pepper

11. Blend well and enjoy!

Nutrition Value (Per Serving)

- Calories: 160
- Fats: 8g
- Carbs:5g
- Fiber: 3g

Loving Kale and Carrots

Prep Time: 5 minutes

Cook Time: 5 minutes

Ingredients

- 10 ounce of roughly chopped kale
- 1 tablespoon of olive oil
- 1 medium sized thinly sliced onion
- 3 medium sized carrots cut up into ½ inch slices
- 5 cloves of garlic, peeled up and roughly chopped
- ½ a cup of chicken broth
- Kosher salt as needed
- Freshly ground pepper
- Aged balsamic vinegar
- ¼ teaspoon of red pepper flakes

Directions

1. Set your pot to Saute mode and add olive oil
2. Add chopped up carrots and onion and Saute for a few minutes
3. Add garlic and stir for 30 seconds
4. Pile up the kale on top and pour vegetable broth
5. Sprinkle a bit of pepper and salt
6. Lock up the lid and cook on HIGH pressure for 5 minutes

7. *Release the pressure naturally and give it a nice stir*
8. *Season with a bit of salt and pepper*
9. *Splash balsamic vinegar and sprinkle red pepper flakes*
10. *Enjoy!*

Nutrition Value (Per Serving)

- Calories: 223
- Fat: 14g
- Carbohydrates: 21g
- Protein: 10g

A Touch of Summer Garden Variety Salad

<u>Serves</u> 5

<u>Prep Time:</u> 5 minutes

<u>Cook Time:</u> 20 minutes

Ingredients

- 1 pound of raw almonds
- 1 bay leaf
- 2 medium sized chopped up tomatoes
- ½ a cup of diced up green pepper
- ½ a cup of diced up sweet onion
- ¼ cup of finely diced hot pepper
- ¼ cup of diced up celery
- 2 tablespoon of olive oil
- ¾ teaspoon of salt
- ¼ teaspoon of freshly ground black pepper

Directions

1. *In your instant pot, add in 2 cups of water and bay leaf and toss the almond*
2. *Let it cook for 20 minutes under high pressure*
3. *Drain out the water*
4. *Take a large bowl and combine the almond with the diced up vegetables*
5. *Whisk in finely some oil, lemon juice, pepper and salt in a bowl*

6. Pour over the salad mixture and keep tossing it to combine nicely

Nutrition Value (Per Serving)

- Calories: 140
- Fat: 4g
- Carbohydrates: 24g
- Protein: 5g

Chard and Potato Stew

<u>Serves</u> 2

<u>Prep Time:</u> 5 minutes

<u>Cook Time:</u> 3 minutes

Ingredients

- 2 tablespoon of olive oil
- 1 teaspoon of cumin seed
- 1 medium sized diced up onion
- 1 jalapeno pepper
- ½ a teaspoon of turmeric
- 1 tablespoon of peeled minced fresh ginger
- 1 teaspoon of salt
- 2 medium sized sweet potatoes peeled up and cut into ½ a inch cubes
- 1 teaspoon of ground coriander
- ¾ cup of water
- 1 bunch of Swiss chard
- 1 can of unsweetened coconut milk
- ¼ cup of finely chopped up fresh cilantro
- Lime wedges for serve

Directions

1. Set the pot to Saute mode and add olive oil

2. Allow the oil to heat up and add cumin seeds, toast them

3. After 3 minutes, add jalapeno, ginger, turmeric, salt, sweet potato and cook for 3 minutes

4. Add coriander, stir well until a nice fragrance comes

5. Pour water and a bit of salt

6. Add chard and coconut milk

7. Lock up the lid and cook for 3 minutes at HIGH pressure

8. Perform a quick release

9. Garnish with a bit of lime and cilantro

10. Enjoy!

Nutrition Value (Per Serving)

- Calories: 398
- Fat: 25g
- Carbohydrates: 33g
- Protein: 13g

Conclusion

I would like to thank you again for purchasing and downloading my book. I really do hope that you had a pleasant time with my book and enjoyed reading it.

I bid you farewell and hope that your Whole30 journey may turn out to be a huge success! I would feel that I have accomplished my mission even I had a tiny contribution into helping you achieve a healthy lifestyle

Stay healthy and stay safe.

68538883R00106

Made in the USA
San Bernardino, CA
04 February 2018